2807   16+

cat

12⁰⁰

GreatestQuarterbacks

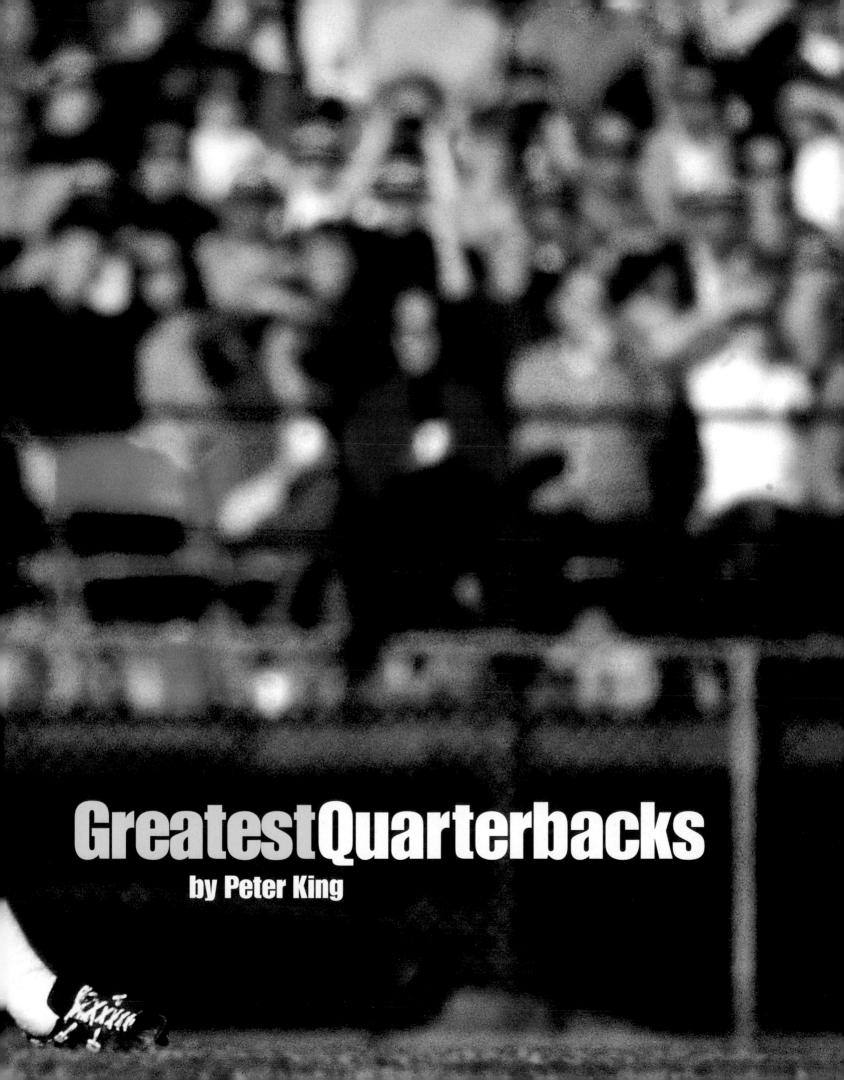

GreatestQuarterbacks
by Peter King

ISBN 1-883013-93-3
Manufactured in the United States of America
First printing 1999

Sports Illustrated Director of New Product Development: STANLEY
WEIL

GREATEST QUARTERBACKS
Project Director: MORIN BISHOP
  Designers: BARBARA CHILENSKAS, JIA BAEK
  Senior Editors: JOHN BOLSTER, EVE PETERSON
  Associate Editors: WARD CALHOUN, THERESA DEAL, JEFF LABRECQUE
  Photography Editor: JOHN S. BLACKMAR

GREATEST QUARTERBACKS was prepared by
Bishop Books, Inc.
611 Broadway
New York, New York 10012

TIME INC. HOME ENTERTAINMENT
President: Stuart Hotchkiss
Executive Director, Branded Businesses: David Arfine
Director, Non Branded Businesses: Alicia Longobardo
Director, Brand Licensing: Risa Turken
Director, Marketing Services: Michael Barrett
Director, Retail & Special Sales: Thomas Mifsud
Associate Directors: Roberta Harris, Kenneth Maehlum
Product Managers: Andre Okolowitz, Niki Viswanathan, Daria Raehse
Associate Product Managers: Dennis Sheehan, Meredith Shelley, Bill
Totten, Lauren Zaslansky
Assistant Product Managers: Victoria Alfonso, Jennifer Dowell, Ann
Gillespie
Licensing Manager: JoAnna West
Associate Licensing Manager: Regina Feiler
Associate Manager, Retail & New Markets: Bozena Szwagulinski
Editorial Operations Director: John Calvano
Book Production Manager: Jessica McGrath
Assistant Book Production Manager: Jonathan Polsky
Book Production Coordinator: Kristen Lizzi
Fulfillment Manager: Richard Perez
Assistant Fulfillment Manager: Tara Schimming
Financial Director: Tricia Griffin
Financial Manager: Robert Dente
Associate Financial Manager: Steven Sandonato
Executive Assistant: Mary Jane Rigoroso

Special thanks to: Emily Rabin and Jennifer Bomhoff

We welcome your comments and suggestions about
SPORTS ILLUSTRATED Books. Please write to us at:
Sports Illustrated Books
Attention: Book Editors
PO Box 11016
Des Moines, IA 50336-1016

If you would like to order any of our Hard Cover Collector Edition
books, please call us at 1-800-327-6388. (Monday through Friday,
7:00 a.m.– 8:00 p.m. or Saturday, 7:00 a.m.–6:00 p.m. Central Time).

10 9 8 7 6 5 4 3 2 1

Contents

Introduction

It will serve you well as you read this book to remember one thing: This isn't baseball. You don't get 3,000 hits and automatically make the King Top Twenty. In the SI pro football world, stats are important, but winning rules.

I adopted this mantra as a beat reporter for *Newsday* in the mid-1980s. During that period of my life, I was like most of you probably are today. In the Alltime NFL Fantasy Draft, chances are you'd take Dan Marino over Otto Graham. Marino's numbers dwarf Graham's because of the different eras in which they played. But Graham leads Marino in pro championships by a touchdown, 7–zip. Seven titles to none. That makes him a better quarterback, in my book—and this *is* my book—than Marino. Period. End of discussion.

To paraphrase Raiders owner Al Davis, "Just win, QB." That's the governing

Contrasting styles: Marino (opposite) may have been the greatest pure passer in history—he holds virtually every meaningful career record; Montana (above) combined intelligence, precision, and mobility to win four Super Bowl titles.

principle of the rankings in this book. That's what I watched Phil Simms do for the Giants in the 1980s. In '84, the year Simms came into his own, coach Bill Parcells made the young quarterback the linchpin of his offense. Simms threw for 4,044 yards, a career high, and the Giants made the playoffs. During the next two seasons, Parcells had an experienced offensive line and an elusive running back, Joe Morris, so he shifted the focus of the offense from Simms to Morris. The Giants won the Super Bowl after the 1986 season. To confound Denver in that game, Parcells put the spotlight

back on Simms. The quarterback responded with a career day, completing 22 of 25 passes—a Super Bowl–record 88%—and the Giants romped, 39–20. "Not every quarterback would be willing to go from being a star to the guy doing what was best for the team," Parcells said a couple of years after Super Bowl XXI. "The best quarterbacks care about one thing—winning."

In this book, we care about several things—performance in the clutch, passing yards, touchdown passes—but none more than winning.

"People don't appreciate Simms now," Parcells

Super Bowl Heroes: Simms (right) and Young (opposite) saved their best performances for the grandest stage of all. Simms was a near-perfect 22-for-25 in New York's 39–20 thrashing of Denver in Super Bowl XXI; Young stepped out of Montana's long shadow by tossing a Super Bowl–record six touchdown passes against San Diego in Super Bowl XXIX.

continued, "but I'll promise you this: You'll miss him when he's gone." And so the Giants have. From 1984, Simms's first season as a full-time starter, to 1993, when he retired, the Giants were 99–57 in non-strike games. Without him, they've gone 38-41-1 (through 1998). The Giants won 63% of their games with Simms as their primary starter. They've won 48% since he left. They won two Super Bowls with him, none without him. His career numbers are relatively modest (33,462 yards passing, 15th alltime entering the 1999 season), but his team averaged 10 wins a year and won

two titles. That's why Simms is higher on our list than you might expect: 20th, which puts him six spots ahead of Warren Moon. Before the '99 season, when he was a backup in Kansas City, Moon had passed for 49,097 yards and 290 touchdowns but no titles.

Which is not to devalue Moon's accomplishments, or his place in history: To rank 27th among the more than 800 quarterbacks in the history of the game is none too shabby. That makes him better than 97% of the men who have played the position, which, by the way, I

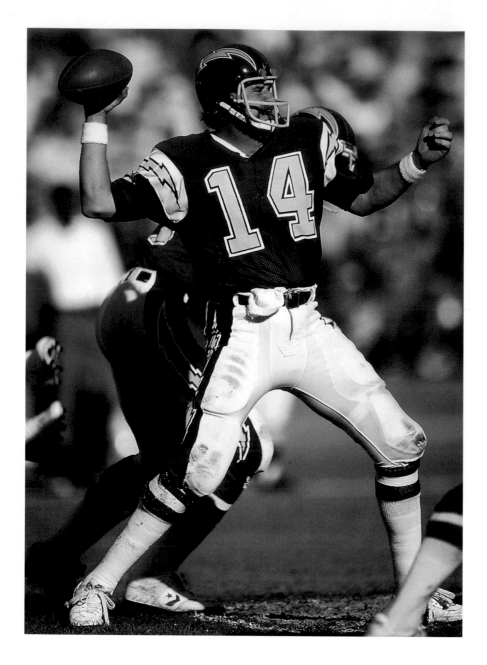

In the NFL in 1998, seven quarterbacks completed as many as six of every 10 throws, on the average. That's considered good, 60% accuracy or better. Of those seven, only four threw twice as many touchdown passes as interceptions and only four played for teams with winning records. A quarterback who does all three—completes 60% of his passes, has a 2:1 touchdown-to-interception ratio and leads his team to a winning record—has had a very good season.

But it doesn't happen very often. In 1998, three NFL quarterbacks turned the trick—San Francisco's Steve Young, the Jets' Vinny Testaverde and Minnesota's Randall Cunningham. In 1997, two did—Young and Jacksonville's Mark Brunell. It's supremely hard to be a great quarterback. And in no other sport do teams spend thousands of man-hours scouting, researching and tape-watching one position the way NFL teams do the quarterback spot.

"The toughest position in sports is sort of a bar discussion that never can be solved," says Peyton Manning, the Indianapolis Colts' quarterback, who will be on this list, bank on it, in 20 years. "But I don't see how it's not quarterback. Point guard is tough, but those guys don't have to deal with crowd noise. Golfers work in silence, pretty much. A pitcher might have a line drive hit back at him, but that's his biggest fear, and it doesn't happen that much. A quarterback can't hear, he's calling a lot of plays at the line, he's got five or six good athletes bigger than he is coming at him every play, and it wears on you to get hit, get hit, get hit, and have to come back and make a play. And you have to make the right decision. One bad throw can lose a game."

And one more thing: "Most of the time," Manning says, "you can't see." The sequoias that are

Bombs Away: Fouts (above), who passed for over 4,000 yards in three straight years, spearheaded one of the most prolific aerial attacks the NFL has ever seen; Namath (opposite) brought credibility to the AFL when he became the first man to break the 4,000-yard passing barrier in 1967.

consider to be the most demanding in sports.

I respect what batters do in baseball, and maybe they're simply getting a lot better these days, but in 1999 53 players hit .300, 45 belted 30 or more home runs, and 59 knocked in 100 or more runs. Golf is a difficult game, one that I am no closer to conquering than when I first started playing, but the ball is stationary, and there's no pass rush. No single position in basketball is significantly more challenging than the others. A hockey or soccer goalkeeper has it tough, but in some games the goalie can record a shutout without being strongly challenged.

linemen in front of you create that handicap.

There's also the pressure of being the focus of attention every Sunday. "Every time you drop back to pass," former Bengals quarterback Boomer Esiason once said, "you've got the eyes of an entire city, state and region on you. That's pretty heavy."

So in ranking the men who withstood this pressure, faced these obstacles, week in, week out, for years, we placed a premium on those who could not only produce in these trying circumstances but also triumph, win championships. Guys like Graham and Joe Montana, then, are in our top flight. Following closely behind them are hugely productive quarterbacks who were great in the clutch but never won a title. Men like Marino, whose career stats and piles of fourth-quarter comebacks are so impressive they place him in the Top Ten. The third group consists of quarterbacks who won titles or racked up prodigious numbers (Terry Bradshaw, Dan Fouts) and quarterbacks who did a little of both (Brett Favre, Joe Namath).

If you don't agree with the rankings just know that I came by them honestly, and feel free to take me up on the subject at a game, or on a talk show, or on a plane.

Nothing like a good football argument.

1-10 : The Elite

1-10: The elite

I can hear it now.

Otto Graham? Are you kidding? Have the bugs from your Powerbook infested your brain and devoured your football intelligence? Sure, we've heard of Graham. Good player, we think. But c'mon. Montana. Unitas. Marino. Those are the names you think of when you think of the alltime greats. Not some guy who played half his career in a minor league. Hand in your SI windbreaker, hack. You're through.

It is, I admit, a controversial call.

It is hard to compete with Dan Marino's 17 years of prolific passing, or John Elway's 16 years of cardiac comebacks. It's difficult to top Joe Montana's 15 years of preternatural cool, or John Unitas's 18 years of revolutionizing the position.

But most of all, it is hard to compete with the modernness of those players. We've witnessed their stardom. We watched Montana drive the length of the field to beat Cincinnati late in Super Bowl XXIII; we watched Elway play valiantly his entire career, then cap it off with consecutive Super Bowl wins over Green Bay and Atlanta. And though Marino hadn't won a title by 1999, we were awed by his lightning release and by his astounding production against corners from Lester Hayes to Charles Woodson. That these legends would be on or near the top of our list was a foregone conclusion.

But Graham didn't have *SportsCenter* or SPORTS ILLUSTRATED or *Monday Night Football* to amplify his achievements. Graham's peak came before the NFL was a fixture in households across America every Sunday. To see him in action we have to look at grainy old footage that may as well have been shot by the Lumière brothers. Yet Graham deserves to be at the top of the list, for a simple reason: He played professional football for 10 years, and he competed in the championship game of his league 10 times, leading his team to victory in seven of those games. Combined with his 23,584 career passing yards (in the still-formative era of the forward pass) and his 174 touchdown passes, this accomplishment makes Otto Graham the clear No. 1. He was all about winning. And rest assured, he could hold his own with the best of today's gunslingers. He threw the puffed-up, more circular ball of his era with tremendous accuracy, and with a spiral tighter than spandex. When the game called for him to win throwing, he won throwing.

When the game called for his calm leadership or for him to hand the ball off to Cleveland's Hall of Fame fullback, Marion Motley, he did so. Whatever it took to win. First in the old All-America Football Conference, later in the NFL when it deigned to admit the Browns, who immediately took the league by storm.

The second spot on our list goes to Montana for his cool, unruffled artistry. Impervious to pressure, he went about his business: a quick out here, a dart down the middle there; whatever was needed for victory, which somehow seemed assured when he was playing. Unitas is third, because of his tremendous play in the clutch and because he was the first prolific passer in history. Old Redskins quarterback Sammy Baugh, who played from 1937 to '52, is fourth, because he led the league in passing three times as a tailback and three times as a quarterback, and he may have been the best all-around player in history. Then comes Elway, the King of the Comeback.

After that there's more room for debate. Maybe the best pure passer of them all, Marino, tops most of the all-time statistical tables and ranks sixth. Arguably the best runner-passer ever, Steve Young, is seventh. Terry Bradshaw, who overcame the worst start to a career of anyone on this list and led the Steelers to four Super Bowl titles, is eighth. The freewheeling Brett Favre, who won three straight MVP awards before turning 30, is ninth, though we reserve the right to revamp our rankings in 10 years and move him up. His star is still rising. Tenth is the artful Roger Staubach, who played his best, always, when games were on the line.

1 OttoGraham

Pro Seasons: 10.
Championship game starts: 10.
Need we say more?

A leader on the sideline (right) and a winner on the field, Graham led the Browns to the NFL championship in 1955, capping his brilliant career with a scoring plunge to ice the victory over the Rams (opposite) in his final pro game.

Former New York Giants general manager George Young first persuaded me of the brilliance of Otto Graham. If you put a premium on winning in your assessment of great players, Young reasoned, "Then how can anyone be better than Otto Graham? All he did was quarterback his team to the championship game 10 straight years."

Indeed Graham did, and to think that he came close to pursuing a career in pro basketball instead of football. In early 1946, having completed a World War II stint as a Navy Air Corps pilot, Graham signed to play with the Rochester Royals of the National Basketball League, a forerunner of the NBA. A winner from the start, he helped the Royals win a league championship that season.

At the same time, a young football coach named Paul Brown was starting a new team in a new league, the All-America Football Conference, and he wanted Graham to be his quarterback. Brown had scouted Graham in football at Northwestern, and he liked what he had seen. "Poise, ball control and leadership," Brown said. "Otto has the basic requirements of a T quarterback."

When he returned to his boyhood home in Waukegan, Ill., in the spring of '46 Graham had a choice to make. Fresh from winning a pro basketball title, he had to decide between basketball and football. He loved football, and he sensed that Brown possessed a dedication to greatness.

Brown, and the Browns, won.

"I made the right choice," Graham said years later.

Talk about an understatement. The quick and powerful Browns were born in 1946 into the AAFC, which was to

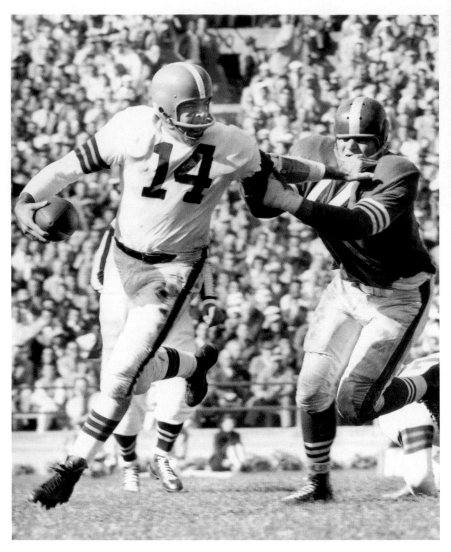

Running Wild: Graham (above), who helped to popularize the passing game, was also effective as a runner; in a 56–10 pounding of Detroit in the 1954 NFL championship game (opposite), Graham ran for three scores and passed for three more.

THE RECORD

YEAR	TEAM	G	ATT	COMP	COMP%	YDS	TD	INT	RATING
1946*	Clev	14	174	95	54.6	1834	17	5	112.1
1947*	Clev	14	269	163	60.6	2753	25	11	109.2
1948*	Clev	14	333	173	52.0	2713	25	15	85.6
1949*	Clev	12	285	161	56.5	2785	19	10	97.5
1950	Clev	12	253	137	54.2	1943	14	20	64.7
1951	Clev	12	265	147	55.3	2205	17	16	79.2
1952	Clev	12	364	181	49.7	2816	20	24	66.6
1953	Clev	12	258	167	64.7	2722	11	9	99.7
1954	Clev	12	240	142	59.2	2092	11	17	73.5
1955	Clev	12	185	98	53.0	1721	15	8	94.0
TOTAL		126	2626	1464	55.8	23,584	174	135	86.6

*From 1946 to '49 Graham and the Browns played in the All-America Football Conference.

> "They should have named them the Cleveland Grahams."
>
> —Buck Shaw,
> *former coach of the Philadelphia Eagles*

Graham

the NFL in the 1940s what the American Football League was to the established league in the '60s. The Browns played AAFC football for four seasons. They went 47-4-3, and won the AAFC title each year. "We were a passing team in the era of the run," Graham said. "But we could still dominate with the run, too. In the morning, at practice, we'd work on the run. In the afternoon, we'd work on the pass. My talents? I could throw hard if I had to, I could lay it up soft, I could drill the sideline pass. I had

the luxury of having the same receivers almost all my career. We developed the timed sideline pass, the comeback route where the receiver goes to the sideline, stops, and comes back to the ball. Everything thrown on rhythm."

That's important to know. Graham was devoted to precision. The son of suburban Chicago music teachers, he didn't dabble in music as an adolescent, he mastered the piano, the violin, the French horn and the cornet. At Northwestern, he was no dumb jock. He majored in

education, minored in music. He was a featured player in the Northwestern orchestra as well as an All-America in football and basketball. Friends and teammates called him a perfectionist.

He was very close to perfect on the football field for a decade. Some fans discount Cleveland's dominance in the AAFC because it was considered inferior to the NFL. Pshaw. That's like throwing out Joe Namath's AFL feats. But if you're of a mind to consider only NFL accomplishments, let's do it. And

In an era dominated by grind-it-out offenses, Graham (above, versus Detroit) routinely threw for at least 2,000 yards per season; Graham rushed for 12 yards in the first quarter of the 1950 title game (opposite), aided by a teammate's in-your-face block on a potential tackler. The Browns went on to win 30–28 on Lou Groza's field goal with 20 seconds remaining in regulation.

let's start with the first game of the 1950s, the first game Cleveland played after being admitted to the league.

NFL commissioner Bert Bell decided to baptize the AAFC champs by fire: He arranged for the Browns to play the defending NFL champion Philadelphia Eagles. The Eagles had allowed 11 points a game while going 11–1 in 1949. Few people believed Cleveland could compete with the Eagles, and the Philadelphia press primed the crowd of 71,237 for a rout by labeling the Browns' running and passing game a "high school offense."

Graham threw touchdown passes in the first, second and third quarters. He ran for a touchdown in the fourth. Cleveland won 35–10. Afterward, Philadelphia coach Greasy Neale griped that the Browns won because they threw so much, not because they were more physical. In a rematch later that season in Cleveland, at coach Brown's insistence, the Browns overpowered the Eagles without throwing a single pass and won 13–7. Three weeks later in the NFL championship game, Graham threw four touchdown passes to lead Cleveland over the Rams 30–28. The "minor leaguers" had won the NFL in their first year in the league.

For the record, Graham's AAFC teams won 89.8 percent of their games,

supportingcast

Never before or since has a professional football team been named for its coach. Yet it seems entirely appropriate that, in 1946, Cleveland's new AAFC franchise should have borne Paul Brown's name. The coach who would eventually be recognized as the father of the modern pro game was wildly popular in his home state of Ohio for having transformed the football team at Massillon High School into a juggernaut with a perenially packed 22,000-seat stadium and then for bringing a national championship to Ohio State in 1942.

In an era when most quarterbacks freelanced more often than not, Brown championed an open, pass-based offense that operated from a formal playbook, one of Brown's many football innovations. He studied opposing teams meticulously and frequently watched his revolutionary pass patterns foil their defenses. An intense perfectionist, he expected the same from his players, who submitted to written tests and graded performances. Brown instituted advanced scouting, the "pocket" to protect the passer, and the use of messenger guards to bring in plays from the sidelines.

In 17 seasons under Brown's intense, focused leadership, Cleveland won 76% of its games, made 13 postseason appearances and took four AAFC and three NFL titles.

his NFL teams 81.3 percent. There's not much more a quarterback can do to help his team win than Graham did.

He had announced that he would retire after the 1954 season, and Cleveland fans gave Graham a standing ovation as he left the field following the Browns' 56–10 drubbing of Detroit for the '54 championship. They had good reason: Graham ran for three scores and passed for three more in the rout. In the locker room after the game, Brown tried to talk Graham out of retiring. No dice, Otto said respectfully; I've had a great run, and now I'm going to sell insurance and run my discount house and stop getting beaten up every week-

end in the fall. A few months later, Brown offered Graham a raise to a league-high $25,000 a year. Graham relented, and so the day after Christmas, 1955, he led the Browns onto the field for their 10th straight championship game, and his last game. They played the Rams in Los Angeles, with a pro-record 85,693 people packing the Coliseum. Long, methodical drives. Two touch-

down passes and 209 passing yards. After three quarters Brown took Graham out of the game and the gigantic crowd rose as one, disappointed for the home team but knowing that the DiMaggio of their sport was jogging off the field for the final time. "Otto Graham," Brown said after the game, "is the greatest player I've ever coached."

That's good enough for us.

2 JoeMontana

The hotter the situation, the cooler Joe Cool became. He was undefeated (4–0) in Super Bowls, and unmatched in the clutch.

Combine matinee idol looks (left) with an uncanny flair for the dramatic and you have the stuff of the Montana legend; in Super Bowl XIX (opposite), Montana's second trip to the title game, he was the MVP once again, passing for 331 yards and three TDs in the Niners' 38–16 victory over Miami.

There is a scene from *Seinfeld* that you might remember. Elaine is interviewing for the editor's job left vacant by the death of Jacqueline Onassis (how does this get into a football book, you ask?) when the subject of Jackie O's grace comes up. Elaine says that she too has a little bit of grace, and the publisher looks at her sternly. "You can't have a little grace," the woman says. "You either have grace, or you don't."

In the rugged world of football, the word grace doesn't crop up too often—and when it does it's usually used to describe a wide receiver, possibly a running back. But Joe Montana had grace. He breathed it. He was NFL royalty, disguised in a spindly-legged, 6'2", body, and powered by only an average NFL arm. But inside his size 7¼ helmet Montana had the brightest bulb that ever burned in a quarterback's cranium. "When you talked to Joe," said his first quarterback coach in the NFL, Sam Wyche, "he didn't just listen. He sucked the knowledge out and kept compiling it in his head,

year after year, so that nothing a defense could ever do to him was a surprise."

Montana also had the one ingredient that every great player in every sport has to have: confidence. This self-assurance was nurtured during his youth in hard-scrabble Monongahela, Pa., a few long spirals from Pittsburgh. Whether he was playing football, basketball or baseball, Montana was expected to succeed. "Every time I played when I was a kid," Montana once said, "there was pressure to win, pressure to be the best."

When he was a freshman at Notre Dame he was seventh on the quarterback depth chart. He became a full-time starter in his junior year. In his senior year, 1978, the Irish trailed Houston by 22 points midway through the fourth quarter of the Cotton Bowl. Montana had the flu, and he had drained three cups of bouillon at halftime to try to warm up. Somehow, he rallied Notre Dame to a 35–34 win. In 1981, he ended the dynasty of the Dallas Cowboys, throwing a last-minute touchdown pass to Dwight Clark that only Clark could have caught to steal the NFC championship game.

"How many people are there in the world, three billion? And how many guys are there who can do what he can do? Him, maybe Marino on a good day. Perhaps God had a hand in this."

—Jeff Petrucci, *Montana's high school quarterback coach*

Blessed with an instinctive sense of where everyone was on the field, Montana (above in the '82 NFC title game against Dallas) was a master at finding an open receiver downfield at the last possible moment; when forced to, he could also run, as on this play (opposite), a 15-yard scramble for a first down that set up San Francisco's first score against Miami in Super Bowl XIX.

He returned from back surgery in 55 days in 1986 to lead the 49ers to the play-offs. He completed 22 passes in a row in 1987. He drove the 49ers 92 yards in the final minutes to beat the Bengals in the Super Bowl after the 1988 season. He led the Niners to four Super Bowl titles in four tries. Will any quarterback ever match Montana's career Super Bowl numbers: 4–0, 68% completion percentage, 11 touchdowns, zero interceptions? The highest career quarterback rating belongs to Steve Young, who had a 97.5

mark after the '98 season. Montana's career Super Bowl rating is 127.8.

"A lot of people have used these numbers to say I played better under pressure," said Montana. "I don't think that's true. Every game I played, I played under pressure. So I don't think it was that I played better under pressure. I think it was that I played the same."

Exclamation point: In Montana's first four full seasons, he completed 63.6% of his passes. In his last four full seasons, he completed 63.3%.

My fondest memory of Montana is from a game you might not recall. Early in 1989, my first year at SI, I was assigned to cover a 49ers-Eagles game, and I met the Niners in Philadelphia. To my surprise, I was allowed to ride the team bus to practice the day before the game, and I saw Montana's jockish leadership firsthand. I sat in the seat behind Montana and Charles Haley, who was napping. Haley awoke in time to see Veterans Stadium pass outside the bus window. "What's that?" he said, nodding to the stadium. Montana, to titters of laughter, said, "That's the stadium we're playing at tomorrow, you dumb ----!" I

THE RECORD

YEAR	TEAM	G	ATT	COMP	COMP%	YDS	TD	INT	RATING
1979	SF	16	23	13	56.5	96	1	0	81.1
1980	SF	15	273	176	64.5	1795	15	9	87.8
1981	SF	16	488	311	63.7	3565	19	12	88.4
1982	SF	9	346	213	61.6	2613	17	11	88.0
1983	SF	16	515	332	64.5	3910	26	12	94.6
1984	SF	16	432	279	64.6	3630	28	10	102.9
1985	SF	15	494	303	61.3	3653	27	13	91.3
1986	SF	8	307	191	62.2	2236	8	9	80.7
1987	SF	13	398	266	66.8	3054	31	13	102.1
1988	SF	14	397	238	59.9	2981	18	10	87.9
1989	SF	13	386	271	70.2	3521	26	8	112.4
1990	SF	15	520	321	61.7	3944	26	16	89.0
1991	DNP								
1992	SF	1	21	15	71.4	126	2	0	118.4
1993	KC	11	298	181	60.7	2144	13	7	87.4
1994	KC	14	493	299	60.6	3283	16	9	83.6
TOTAL		192	5391	3409	63.2	40,551	273	139	92.3

Montana

Even at 6' 2", Montana had to struggle to get the ball over NFL behemoths such as 6' 9" Ed (Too Tall) Jones (left); Montana signaling a score (above) became one of the most familiar sights in football during his 15 seasons in the league.

don't know about you, but I would never call Charles Haley, one of the biggest and toughest men in the NFL, anything but "Sir." I figured Montana must have been pretty comfortable with his status on the Niners and with his teammates to venture that jab.

In any case, Montana was incredible the next day. He absorbed brutal hits from Seth Joyner and Reggie White in the first half, and the rising-star Eagles led by 11 points in the fourth quarter. Back came Montana, throwing three touchdown passes in four minutes, an incredible comeback win on the road. Afterward, Montana played down everything he'd done. "I played okay," he said. That isn't what the 49ers owner thought. After the game, a bawling Eddie DeBartolo Jr., hugged Montana and said, "I love you Joe! You're the greatest!"

So we saw.

inSI'swords

Because Montana made quarterbacking look so stylish and so natural, it was tempting to assume his life would be empty when he retired. What seems to be happening instead is that Montana, by virtue of his uncomplicated manner, is deriving stimulation from life's basic pleasures....

After 15 NFL seasons, 40,551 passing yards, 273 touchdown passes, three Super Bowl MVP awards, two regular-season MVPs and millions of dollars from football and endorsements, Montana is, in every sense of the term, set for life. He has his family: wife Jennifer; daughters Alexandra, 9, and Elizabeth, 8; and sons Nathaniel, 5, and Nicholas, 3. He has his parents close by, Joe Sr. and Theresa having moved from the western Pennsylvania steel town of Monongahela almost a decade ago to be near their only child.... He has a single-engine airplane and a 14 handicap he would like to bring down into single digits. He has a host of new hobbies, including archery, and a soon-to-be-announced affiliation with a major IndyCar team. He has broadcasting discussions in the works with NBC, Fox, ESPN and Turner. He has long-term endorsement contracts and sound investments. He has his health and he has his legend.
—Michael Silver, April 24, 1995

3 JohnnyUnitas

Played in championship games in the 1950s, '60s and '70s. First to pass for 40,000 career yards

Throughout his career, regardless of the opponent, Unitas (above, versus the Packers in 1966 and opposite, versus the Raiders in the 1971 AFC title game) was ever cool, ever in control, ever the winner.

You want clutch? This is clutch:

Baltimore Colts versus New York Giants. First nationally televised NFL championship game. Dec. 28, 1958, Yankee Stadium. Cold. Giants leading 17–14. Two minutes to play. Baltimore ball at its own 14. Third and 10. Fans howling, knowing one defensive stand by their team anytime in the next 60 yards wins the game.

John Unitas, three years removed from sandlot football under a railroad trestle in a tough neighborhood of Pittsburgh, stepped under center for the Colts. He

barked the signals. He could see his breath, and he could see the snorting exhalations of 11 grizzled Giants across the line of scrimmage. Unitas took the snap and retreated. In a second he saw Lenny Moore open five yards upfield and drilled one to him between the numbers, good for 11 yards and the first down. On the next play Unitas threw a laser to Raymond Berry on a slant pattern for 25 yards. Then Berry again, diving low, for 15. Berry a third time, on a classic button-hook, drilled between the numbers, to the Giants 13-yard line.

"Unitas to Berry, Unitas to Berry," former Giants linebacker Sam Huff said a couple of years ago. "After 40 years, it still rings in my ears." The crowd groaned as Steve Myrha's field goal sent the game into overtime. In the extra session Unitas did it again—13 plays, 80 yards. He confounded the Giants by lofting one to little-known tight end Jim Mutscheller to bring the Colts to the Giants' one. The drive ended on a one-yard plunge by Alan Ameche, and the Colts were NFL champions.

"Never thought it was much of a game, until the last two minutes," Unitas said years later.

THE RECORD

YEAR	TEAM	G	ATT	COMP	COMP%	YDS	TD	INT	RATING
1956	Balt	12	198	110	55.6	1498	9	10	74.0
1957	Balt	12	301	172	57.1	2550	24	17	88.0
1958	Balt	10	263	136	51.7	2007	19	7	90.0
1959	Balt	12	367	193	52.6	2899	32	14	92.0
1960	Balt	12	378	190	50.3	3099	25	24	73.7
1961	Balt	14	420	229	54.5	2990	16	24	66.1
1962	Balt	14	389	222	57.1	2967	23	23	76.5
1963	Balt	14	410	237	57.8	3481	20	12	89.7
1964	Balt	14	305	158	51.8	2824	19	6	96.4
1965	Balt	11	282	164	58.2	2530	23	12	97.4
1966	Balt	14	348	195	56.0	2748	22	24	74.0
1967	Balt	14	436	255	58.5	3428	20	16	83.6
1968	Balt	5	32	11	34.4	139	2	4	30.1
1969	Balt	13	327	178	54.4	2342	12	20	64.0
1970	Balt	14	321	166	51.7	2213	14	18	65.1
1971	Balt	13	176	92	52.3	942	3	9	52.3
1972	Balt	8	157	88	56.1	1111	4	6	70.8
1973	SD	5	76	34	44.7	471	3	7	40.1
TOTAL		211	5186	2830	54.6	40,239	290	253	78.2

Although sometimes blessed with talented running backs such as Lenny Moore (left, 24) behind him, when in trouble Unitas was always willing to drop back (above) and seek salvation through the air.

Unitas

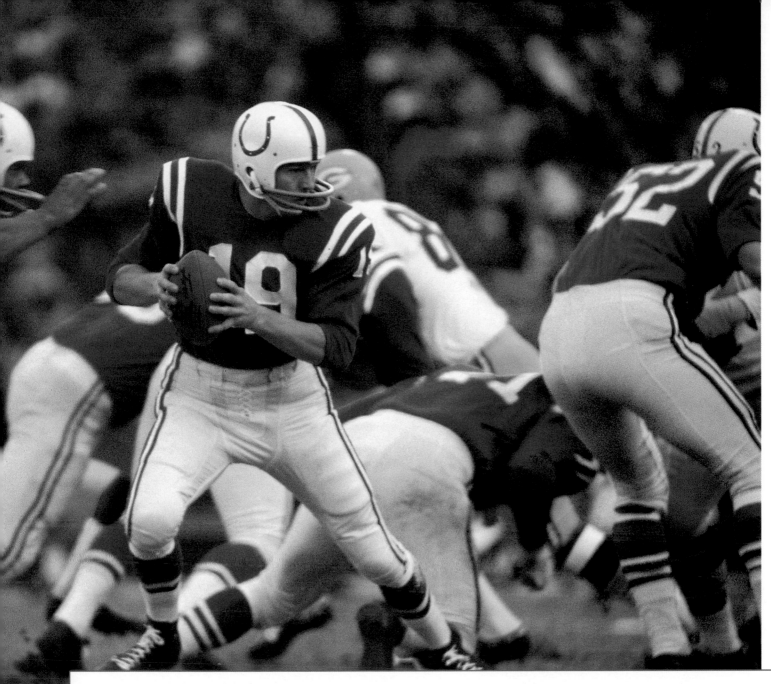

"A lot of people look back and say if we'd covered Ray Berry better that day, we'd have won. Not true. It was Unitas. If we'd stopped Berry, Unitas would've done the same thing with Lenny Moore. Unitas was great that day."

—Sam Huff, *former Giants linebacker on the 1958 championship game*

Maybe so, but the game is routinely tabbed as the greatest in NFL history, and Unitas's performance—in a championship game, mind you—was huge. He drove Baltimore the length of the field for the tying field goal. Then he drove the Colts the length of the field, in sudden death, for the winning touchdown. In his most significant game to that point, Unitas had his biggest day, completing 26 of 40 passes for 349 yards.

Unitas himself was never particularly mobile, but his career had legs. He played for titles in three decades, during which time the league, not to mention society, changed drastically. And his long, strange trip had a very unlikely beginning. He weighed 145 pounds as a high school senior, so the top college teams bypassed him. He went to Louisville, where he was a star, but still

drew only slight interest from the pros. His hometown Pittsburgh Steelers selected him in the ninth round of the 1955 NFL draft. But the Steelers cut him during training camp. Unitas hitch-hiked home from camp, two hours away.

He worked that summer and fall on a construction crew, and played a game a week for the semipro Bloomfield Rams, earning $6 a game. Then the Colts came calling with an offer to attend their training camp in 1956 for the league-minumum salary. Unitas made the team but was initially the backup QB. When Baltimore's starter, George Shaw, went down with a knee injury in the fourth game of the year, Unitas got the job and, quite literally by accident, one of the greatest careers in NFL history began. One group of writers voted Unitas MVP of the league in '57. He took the Colts to the championship in '58 and '59. He won three MVP awards over a nine-year span (1959, '64, '67), and played in five championship games over a 13-year period, from 1958 to '70.

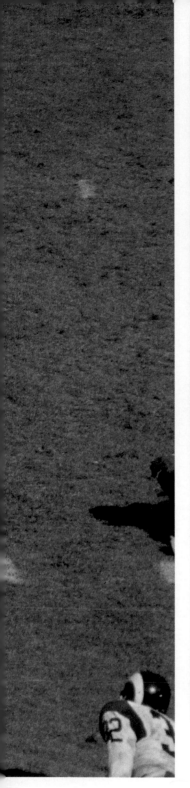

inSI'swords

Unitas became synonymous with toughness on the field, for stepping up in the teeth of the rush and delivering the ball. "I often thought that sometimes he'd hold the ball one count longer than he had to," Los Angeles Rams defensive tackle Merlin Olsen once said, "just so he could take the hit and laugh in your face."

"I kept a picture of Johnny U. over my bed," [Joe] Namath once said. "To me he meant one thing—toughness."

How did Unitas change the game? He was the antithesis of the highly drafted, highly publicized young quarterback. He developed a swagger, a willingness to gamble. He showed that anyone with basic skills could beat the odds if he wanted to succeed badly enough and was willing to work.
—Paul Zimmerman, August 17, 1998

As pro football assumed a larger place in the American consciousness, Unitas became the game's icon, with his stooped and loping stride back from center, his black, high-top football shoes and his Marlboro-Man cool. He also had grit and a rifle of an arm and a seeming inability at any point of any game to get flustered. From 1956 to '60, when defense and the run still dominated the NFL, he threw for a touchdown pass in 47 consecutive games. That may not seem remarkable at first glance, but consider that career touchdown-pass leader Dan Marino's longest streak ever was 30 games. That puts it in perspective.

Unitas looked the same in defeat as in victory, a slope-shouldered but determined sort who never met a challenge he didn't like, or couldn't conquer.

"I don't know what he uses for blood," said Hall of Fame coach Sid Gillman. "But whatever it is, I guarantee you it isn't warm. It's ice cold."

4 SammyBaugh

The versatile Slingin' Sammy led the NFL in passing six times, and remains the alltime career punting leader as well

Baugh (left, in 1938 and opposite, passing versus Washington in '42) was the epitome of toughness throughout his 16-year career, rarely missing action due to injury, in spite of being a full-time two-way player.

This book is about quarterbacks, but former Redskins signal-caller Sammy Baugh is included in it partly for what he did in 1943 as a punter and a defensive back. In '43 Baugh simply had the greatest year ever, by any football player. In additon to leading the NFL in passing (he threw 23 touchdown passes in 10 games), he topped the league in punting, with a record 45.9 yards-per-punt average, and in interceptions, with 11—including four in one game.

Baugh still leads the career punting list, and his versatility will certainly go unmatched in this era of specialization. He won six passing titles in 16 years,

completed 70.3% of his passes in 1945—a higher percentage than Joe Montana ever produced in a season—and played in five championship games, winning two. All this despite the Redskins' maddening tendency to change coaches; Baugh played for eight.

"Sammy Baugh is the best player ever," said Sid Luckman, Baugh's contemporary and a Hall of Fame quarterback himself. "No one will ever equal him."

Yet most contemporary fans don't know a thing about him. At 6' 2" and 180 pounds, Baugh was fairly tall for a quarterback in those days, but still rail-thin. Players of his era wore leather hel-

Baugh

A supremely talented passer (left), Baugh was also a demon on defense; his interception in the end zone (opposite) ended Chicago's fourth-quarter scoring threat in the Redskins' 14–6 title game victory over the Bears in 1942.

THE RECORD

YEAR	TEAM	G	ATT	COMP	COMP%	YDS	TD	INT	RATING
1937	Wash	11	171	81	47.4	1127	8	14	50.5
1938	Wash	9	128	63	49.2	853	5	11	48.1
1939	Wash	9	96	53	55.2	518	6	9	52.3
1940	Wash	11	177	111	62.7	1367	12	10	85.6
1941	Wash	11	193	106	54.9	1236	10	19	52.2
1942	Wash	11	225	132	58.7	1524	16	11	82.5
1943	Wash	10	239	133	55.6	1754	23	19	78.0
1944	Wash	8	146	82	56.2	849	4	8	59.4
1945	Wash	8	182	128	70.3	1669	11	4	109.9
1946	Wash	11	161	87	54.0	1163	8	17	54.2
1947	Wash	12	354	210	59.3	2938	25	15	92.0
1948	Wash	12	315	185	58.7	2599	22	23	78.3
1949	Wash	12	255	145	56.9	1903	18	14	81.2
1950	Wash	11	166	90	54.2	1130	10	11	68.1
1951	Wash	12	154	67	43.5	1104	7	17	43.8
1952	Wash	7	33	20	60.6	152	2	1	79.4
TOTAL		**165**	**2995**	**1693**	**56.5**	**21,886**	**187**	**203**	**72.2**

> ## "Sammy Baugh was the greatest player ever. No one will ever equal him."
>
> —Sid Luckman

mets with no face masks. They wore thigh pads, thin knee pads and cardboard-thin shoulder pads. Baugh sported black hightops. He never shied away from contact, regularly lowering his shoulder into bigger, oncoming lineman. Sometimes, he or his trainer had to pop one of his shoulders back into place during games. He was always asked to play 60 minutes. He never asked out of the lineup once in his 16-year career. Fans of the day loved him because he was a man's man; despite the punishment of being involved in every play, on both sides of the ball, he had a longer career than anyone else in the first 35 years of the NFL. And there was a bit of myth to him. He loved his North Texas ranch so much that his wife would bring their station wagon to the final Redskins game each fall, the car packed, the kids in the back seat. When the game ended Baugh would get in the driver's seat and begin the three- or four-day drive back to the Lone Star State. His teammates wouldn't see him until training camp the next year. Baugh spent the offseasons with his family, working the farm. "There's no better place to live and work than Texas," he would say.

In December 1937, as a 23-year-old rookie who'd seen snow for the first time just three weeks earlier, Baugh led Washington onto Chicago's frozen Wrigley Field for the NFL title game against the Bears. In the early going Baugh suffered what now would be called a hip pointer after being piled on by four Chicago players in the backfield. Somehow, he also sliced open the palm of his throwing hand on the play. He never told the trainer about either injury. All he did on the wind-whipped, frosted field was pass for 354 yards, an NFL championship

Though known for his powerful arm, Baugh was not averse to using his legs when necessary, as on this running play against Chicago in the 1942 title game; a devout family man, Baugh brought his oldest two sons, Todd (opposite, left) and Davey, north from their home in Sweetwater, Texas, to see him play in 1949.

game record. He threw three touchdown passes in a 15-minute span of the second half and Washington won 28–21.

Five years later he did it again, leading his 10–1 Redskins over the 11–0 Bears, the league's only unbeaten team, in the 1942 title game. Baugh threw for the winning touchdown pass, a 38-yarder to Wilbur Moore, and intercepted Sid Luckman once as Washington won 14–6. He punted for a 52.5-yard average in the game, including several quick-kicks into the wind. "He tackled that wind like a sailor," the Bears' legendary coach, George Halas, said years later.

aftermath

Sammy Baugh never doubted for a minute what he would do after his 16 years as a Washington Redskin: leave the limelight and hightail it back to his remote 7,500-acre Texas ranch. As he has said, "I spent half my life away from home playing football and I said that when I finished I would never leave here." Now, at age 85, Baugh is still at that ranch enjoying the good, simple life. He plays golf five days a week—just about a scratch player by his own account—tends his cattle and plays armchair quarterback from Saturday morning through Monday night. Until he tore up his knee in middle age, Baugh was a near-world-class rodeo calf-roper.

The NFL's 75th anniversary celebrations in 1994 nudged the charismatic, tough talking Texan back into the limelight. But Baugh is baffled by the piles of fan mail he now receives from kids who never knew him as a player and wastes little if any time considering offers from promoters and the Redskins organization. If someone wants to drive the dusty Texas backroads to visit with him, that's fine. But, as he put it in 1994, "I'm 80-goddamn-years-old, and I'm happy right where I am."

Baugh is a charter member of the NFL Hall of Fame and was selected as one of the quarterbacks on the alltime, All-America football team by the Football Writers Association of America.

"That game was the disappointment of a lifetime."

Baugh's longevity is all the more remarkable when you consider the rules under which he played. When he broke into the NFL, it was legal for defensive players to hit the quarterback long after he released the ball, as long as the play was still going on. You know what that meant: open season on quarterbacks, with late hits, clotheslines, chops at the knees, pops under the eyes. Baugh loved it, every minute.

"I was never seriously hurt in football," Baugh said when his career ended. "The only time I got hurt was when I got a broken rib from a young steer's horn."

And durability remains Baugh's trademark. As of this printing he is 85 years old, healthy as a horse, and living and working on his ranch in Rotan, Texas.

5 JohnElway

He won two Super Bowls and more games (148) than any other quarterback ever

The Elway intensity (opposite) was rewarded in Super Bowl XXXII, when the Broncos and Elway, losers in three previous trips to the championship game, finally came away on top with a 31–24 win over Green Bay; Elway's celebration (left) warmed hearts all across the nation.

In 1981 the New York Yankees signed an outfield prospect out of Stanford named John Elway. He threw righthanded, batted left. In the NCAA Central Regional tournament, he hit .444 and made the all-tournament team. The Yankees vice president for baseball operations at the time, Bill Bergesch, said of Elway, "We project him as a superstar. He's made for Yankee Stadium. He's big and strong, he can hit with power, and he's got that strong arm. Unfortunately, we are also aware that John has some talent in football...."

Yes, and Vince Lombardi had some talent in coaching; Jim Brown could run the ball. Elway had some talent—let's see—for throwing the ball, for leading a team, for running the ball and for winning. In other words, for quarterbacking.

The Yankees would have to find another superstar, of course. Elway chose football. How history might have been changed had the Yankees thrown astronomical bonus money at Elway. Imagine Elway as the Yankees rightfielder of the late century instead of, say, Paul O'Neill. It doesn't seem so farfetched, actually. But imagine another quarterback running Dan Reeves' and Mike Shanahan's teams in Denver. Maybe Neil Lomax or Todd Blackledge or Tommy Kramer. Just doesn't

fit. Denver without Elway is like Colorado without the Rocky Mountains. And if John had opted for Yankee Stadium instead of Mile High, we football fans would have missed some pretty big thrills.

Upon Elway's retirement in 1999, former coach and offensive specialist Sid Gillman said, "History will treat John kindly, because he could do every-

thing a quarterback has ever needed to do, and he could do it all great."

His talents were not limited to the football field, either. Elway was the classic late-century quarterback: media savvy, possessed of a matinee idol's charisma, and a solid family man to boot. On the field, he had a howitzer for an arm, the instinct to know when

Whether conducting The Drive against Cleveland in 1987 (opposite) or leading the Broncos to victory over Pittsburgh in the 1998 playoffs (left), Elway always possessed preternatural poise in the clutch.

THE RECORD

YEAR	TEAM	G	ATT	COMP	COMP%	YDS	TD	INT	RATING
1983	Den	11	259	123	47.5	1663	7	14	54.9
1984	Den	15	380	214	56.3	2598	18	15	76.8
1985	Den	16	605	327	54.0	3891	22	23	70.2
1986	Den	16	504	280	55.6	3485	19	13	79.0
1987	Den	12	410	224	54.6	3198	19	12	83.4
1988	Den	15	496	274	55.2	3309	17	19	71.4
1989	Den	15	416	223	53.6	3051	18	18	73.7
1990	Den	16	502	294	58.6	3526	15	14	78.5
1991	Den	16	451	242	53.7	3253	13	12	75.4
1992	Den	12	316	174	55.1	2242	10	17	65.7
1993	Den	16	551	348	63.2	4030	25	10	92.8
1994	Den	14	494	307	62.1	3490	16	10	85.7
1995	Den	16	542	316	58.3	3970	26	14	86.4
1996	Den	15	466	287	61.6	3328	26	14	89.2
1997	Den	16	502	280	55.8	3635	27	11	87.5
1998	Den	13	356	210	59.0	2806	22	10	93.0
TOTAL		234	7250	4123	56.9	51,475	300	226	79.9

to run, and an uncanny ability to improvise. No quarterback won more games. No quarterback had more come-from-behind wins. And as the years pass, more times than not Elway will be the answer to the question, If you could pick any quarterback in history for your team with the game on the line, who would it be?

After the events of January 11, 1987, how could it be anyone but Elway? Burned into the memory of Browns fans, that was the day the Broncos played Cleveland for the AFC title and a trip to Super Bowl XXI. And Elway pulled a Unitas. With 5:32 left in regulation, Denver had the ball at its own two-yard line, trailing 20–13. Elway gathered his team around him, hoping to save the Denver season. Fat chance. On two previous fourth-quarter possessions, the Broncos had driven nine and six yards, and the Cleveland crowd, anticipating the first Super Bowl appearance in franchise history, was going bonkers. After-

"You could see it in his eyes; he was ready. It was one of those times you just have to stop yourself and watch the best quarterback ever do his thing."

—Jeff Lewis, *Broncos' backup quarterback on Elway's demeanor before Super Bowl XXXII*

ward, the Broncos would marvel at the wide-eyed, insane spirit of the fans. Elway said these 10 soothing words in the huddle: "If you work hard, good things are going to happen."

A short pass to Sammy Winder, three short running plays, an 11-yard scramble, a 22-yard flat pass to Steve Sewell followed by a 12-yarder to Steve Watson, and the Broncos had reached the Cleveland 40. There was 1:59 left. The tying score appeared within reach. Then an incompletion. Then a sack for an eight-yard loss. Now it looked bleak. Browns fans could smell blood, bellowing, shaking Cleveland Stadium to its foundations, probably rippling nearby Lake Erie.

The Broncos lined up in the shotgun formation. Third-and-18, and his team unable to hear in the din, Elway went to the silent snap count, stomping his right leg up and down to start the two-second count. Problem was, Watson was late going in motion from left to right, and just as he passed between the center and Elway, the ball was snapped. It hit Watson flush on the tush.

And it bounced … right into Elway's hands. (Was it his day or what?)

"Game of inches, huh?" Elway would say later.

He unleashed a 20-yard laser to Mark Jackson. Complete. Elway got the touchdown on a five-yard strike to Jackson, then drove the Broncos to the winning field goal in overtime.

"I felt like a baseball catcher," Jackson said, speaking of the tying score. "That was a John Elway fastball, outside and low."

Don't tell the Yankees. Not that they need him, but they could probably find a place for a guy like Elway.

Elway

Elway (left and above, versus the Chargers and the Giants, respectively, in the 1989 regular season) had the speed to elude would-be tacklers and, at 6' 3" and 215 pounds, the size to run through them as well.

in SI's words

More than any athlete since Wilt Chamberlain on the Philadelphia and San Francisco Warriors of the late 1950s and early '60s, Elway has had to play at a superb level game after game, year after year, to make his team a winner. Though usually surrounded by a human rummage sale, Elway has won more games as a starter than any other quarterback in NFL history (138). It's the equivalent of carving Mount Rushmore with a spoon or composing Beethoven's Ninth on a kazoo.

But Elway's career has been about more than just winning. It has been about escaping defeat half a page from the end of the novel, leaping over pits of fire with the microdot hidden in his cigarette lighter. On first down Elway was "pretty average," his Stanford coach Paul Wiggin once said. But when the elementary school kids are being held hostage and the detonator reads 00:03, who would you rather have clipping the wires than Elway? He may be the only quarterback in history who could stand on his own two-yard line, trailing by five with less than two minutes to play, no timeouts left, windchill -5 [degrees], and cause the opposing coach to mutter, "We're in trouble."
—Rick Reilly, February 4, 1998

6 DanMarino

With his lightning-quick release and deadly accuracy, Marino is the most prolific passer of all time

Marino's record in the playoffs has been a litany of frustration, with Buffalo a frequent source of angst; in 1991 (right), the Bills defeated the Dolphins 44–34 in a snowy shootout, and in '93 (opposite) Buffalo emerged triumphant again, 29–10.

In the first quarter of a 1995 game between the Dolphins and New England in Miami, Dan Marino completed a pass to Irving Fryar to break Fran Tarkenton's career passing record of 47,003 yards. The Dolphins stopped the game and awarded the ball to Marino, by then an icon in South Florida. Miami went on to lose 34–17 but after the game Marino was surrounded by anxious reporters, who wanted tidbits about how he felt when he broke the hallowed record. I witnessed this. Marino had nothing much to say, which, particularly after a loss, was not surprising.

But he did something very telling.

"He's a phenom. There couldn't have been a better passer ever. I mean, the guy just doesn't miss."

—Bruce Smith,
Buffalo defensive end

Arm for the Ages: Marino (left in 1989 and right in '93) has racked up record-breaking passing numbers against every sort of defense coaches have devised.

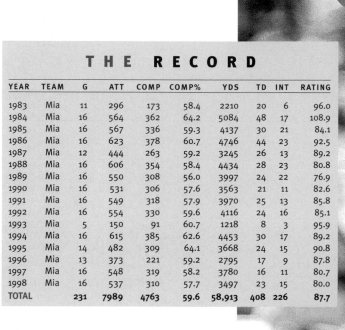

THE RECORD

YEAR	TEAM	G	ATT	COMP	COMP%	YDS	TD	INT	RATING
1983	Mia	11	296	173	58.4	2210	20	6	96.0
1984	Mia	16	564	362	64.2	5084	48	17	108.9
1985	Mia	16	567	336	59.3	4137	30	21	84.1
1986	Mia	16	623	378	60.7	4746	44	23	92.5
1987	Mia	12	444	263	59.2	3245	26	13	89.2
1988	Mia	16	606	354	58.4	4434	28	23	80.8
1989	Mia	16	550	308	56.0	3997	24	22	76.9
1990	Mia	16	531	306	57.6	3563	21	11	82.6
1991	Mia	16	549	318	57.9	3970	25	13	85.8
1992	Mia	16	554	330	59.6	4116	24	16	85.1
1993	Mia	5	150	91	60.7	1218	8	3	95.9
1994	Mia	16	615	385	62.6	4453	30	17	89.2
1995	Mia	14	482	309	64.1	3668	24	15	90.8
1996	Mia	13	373	221	59.2	2795	17	9	87.8
1997	Mia	16	548	319	58.2	3780	16	11	80.7
1998	Mia	16	537	310	57.7	3497	23	15	80.0
TOTAL		231	7989	4763	59.6	58,913	408	226	87.7

When the media horde faded away, Miami's super-efficient P.R. man, Harvey Green, leaned over to Marino and handed him an official play-by-play sheet from the game. "Thought you'd like to have this," Green said.

"What is it?" Marino said, annoyed.

"The play-by-play from the game," Green said. "Thought you'd want it for a souvenir of the day."

"Pfffffff," came the sound out of Marino's mouth. Translation: Who cares about stats? We lost the damn game!

This always was the essence of Marino, who broke just about every passing record there was, without ever truly caring about the milestones. "I never played the game for numbers," he said. "I played the game to win."

A cruel irony, then, that Marino had never won it all as he entered the twilight of his career. He's the Ted Williams of football: a marvel of consistent and enduring excellence. The Drew Bled-soes and Peyton Mannings of the league will have to maintain their current pace into their late 30s to equal Marino's career numbers. Dan the Man holds every major NFL career quarterbacking record—for completions, attempts, yards and touchdowns. I was stunned when I compared 30-year-old Brett Favre's career with Marino's at the same age. Statistically, it was no contest. I had thought of Favre as a player who could break some of Marino's records, but he'll have to have a heck of a run in his 30s to do so. Check out the comparison, at age 30, of the two future Hall of Famers:

Completions: Marino, 2,511–2,390.

Yards: Marino, 31,830–27,728.

Touchdowns: Marino, 245–218.

But then there's Marino's albatross, his white whale: the Vince Lombardi Trophy. He's never hoisted it, and that's why Marino isn't higher on our list. He got to the Super Bowl once, in 1984, when he was a 23-year-old, second-year pro who had thrown an NFL–record 48 touchdown passes during the regular season. The Dolphins tore up the AFC that year, going 14–2, but met a more balanced 49ers team in the Super Bowl and were thoroughly outplayed, losing, 38–16. After 1998, Marino was 7–9 for his career in playoff games, many of which saw opposing defenses concentrate all of their efforts on stopping the

Marino

Miami QB. Too often, Marino's supporting cast was a pedestrian bunch. Stop Marino, the thinking went, and you've won the game.

That was the problem over the years for Miami. Marino was so great that his coach for most of his career, Don Shula, may have relied on him too much, making his team too one-dimensional. In Marino's greatest year, '84, the leading Dolphins rusher was Andra Franklin, who averaged 3.3 yards per carry and gained 746 yards. In the '90s, Marino's leading men in the backfield, in chronological order, were Sammie Smith, Mark Higgs, Bernie Parmalee and Karim Abdul-Jabbar. Not a franchise back among them. Not a 1,000-yard back among them until Abdul-Jabbar in 1996 (1,116).

The Dolphins always began the season saying the running game would be a priority, but when November came, the ball went into Marino's hands. In 1995, as Miami challenged for the AFC East title, Marino threw 34 or more passes in eight of the Dolphins' last 9 games. Miami went 5–4. The Dolphins settled for the wild-card, traveled to Buffalo, where Marino threw 64 times and the Bills won 37–22.

It says here that the lack of a championship should significantly affect but not ruin Marino's standing in history. He was the prototypical drop-back quarterback. Scowling at linemen, decoding defenses, releasing his passes in an eyeblink and demanding excellence from his teammates—Marino is a figure none of us will ever forget. Nor will his foes.

"Playing against Marino twice a year," said Buffalo defensive end Bruce Smith, "is like playing against DiMaggio all the time."

Protected by a strong offensive line and aided by perhaps the quickest release in football history, Marino (above in 1985 and opposite in '84) has rarely had to take a sack.

Marino

in SI's words

Oh, Marino has been controlled on occasion—for a quarter, a half maybe. Then things seem to explode in what defensive coaches have come to call The Frenzy. The ball comes off Marino's hand like a rocket. The Marks Brothers, those two fine wideouts Mark Duper and Mark Clayton, start gobbling up the yardage in huge chunks, 20-yard turn-ins, 30-yard fades, ups, goes. The defense drops off in double coverage and one of the tight ends,

Joe Rose or Bruce Hardy, breaks one down the middle, or halfback Tony Nathan catches a little circle pass and races for 20 yards through a deserted zone. Everything is timed, everything delivered in rhythm in an incredibly short time, and right on the money. The defense becomes unhinged, glassy-eyed— zone, blitz, double zone, it doesn't matter. The Frenzy is on and every drive produces a score. It's like an adding machine gone wild, and a

tight game becomes a blowout. Afterward you ask the defensive coach, "How do you stop Marino?" He'll tell you that the rush has to get to him . . . or you have to disrupt his rhythm and make him wait too long and choke on the ball . . . or your linebackers have to pop up in unexpected places. And then the coach will give a wan smile and say, "We sure as hell couldn't do it."
—Paul Zimmerman, January 21, 1985

7 SteveYoung

The quick feet of Young (opposite, outrunning a Tampa Bay pursuer in 1993), produced a raft of victory celebrations like the one above after a win over New Orleans in 1992.

The evening of January 29, 1995, is one I will never forget. The scene was Joe Robbie Stadium in Miami, the occasion was Super Bowl XXIX. It seems as vivid now as it was when it happened.

THE GAME

Steve Young, exposing a weak San Diego defense, is a maestro, throwing a Super Bowl–record six touchdown passes (that should stand for a while) and evading the rush as deftly as a matador. He decimates the Chargers' defense, pure and simple. This was the game Young had to win. Just had to. You see, Joe Montana, Young's onetime rival for the starting job in San Francisco, had

taken the 49ers to four Super Bowls. Young had led Niners to successful regular seasons but no titles. The ABC cameras zoomed in on Young on the sideline late in the game, which the Niners won in a rout, 49–26, and he was bent over, giggling, pointing to his back. Later, San Francisco tackle Harris Barton said that Young was screaming: "Take that monkey off my back! That monkey shouldn't be there anymore!"

THE LOCKER ROOM.

I worked part-time for ABC then, so I was in the locker room when the door burst open and the 49ers poured in. The commissioner presented the

His propensity to take off often put Young (above, in 1992) in the way of vicious hits like the one delivered by Tampa Bay's Warren Sapp (opposite) in 1997.

THE RECORD

YEAR	TEAM	G	ATT	COMP	COMP%	YDS	TD	INT	RATING
1985	TB	5	138	72	52.2	935	3	8	56.9
1986	TB	14	363	195	53.7	2282	8	13	65.5
1987	SF	8	69	37	53.6	570	10	0	120.8
1988	SF	11	101	54	53.5	680	3	3	72.2
1989	SF	10	92	64	69.6	1001	8	3	120.8
1990	SF	6	62	38	61.3	427	2	0	92.6
1991	SF	11	279	180	64.5	2517	17	8	101.8
1992	SF	16	402	268	66.7	3465	25	7	107.0
1993	SF	16	462	314	68.0	4023	29	16	101.5
1994	SF	16	461	324	70.3	3969	35	10	112.8
1995	SF	11	447	299	66.9	3200	20	11	92.3
1996	SF	12	316	214	67.7	2410	14	6	97.2
1997	SF	15	356	241	67.7	3029	19	6	104.7
1998	SF	15	517	322	62.3	4170	36	12	101.1
TOTAL		166	4065	2622	64.5	32,678	229	103	97.5

Lombardi Trophy, then announcer Brent Musberger grabbed Young to get him to the podium. And Young hugged the piece of sterling silver to his chest as if it were his long-lost collie. And he put his head down, his cheek against the trophy, looking very much like he would never let it go. He held up the NFL's Holy Grail for all to see. Then in a hoarse voice Young gave the team its postgame speech. Not George Seifert, the coach, but Young, the quarterback, summed things up for the team after it had won its record fifth Super Bowl title.

"There were times this was hard!" he shouted, his voice sounding like it would desert him altogether at any moment. "But this is the greatest feeling in the world! No one—*no one*—can ever take this away from us! No one! Ever! It's ours!"

Young did interviews for two hours, after which, nearly dehydrated, he ate a sugar cookie and drank his third can of Gatorade. When he got into his limo to return to the hotel he vomited all over the shoes of his agent, Leigh Steinberg. "Well," said Steinberg, "I'll never wash those shoes again."

Young

THE HOTEL.

In Young's two-room Miami Airport Marriott suite, at 1:15 a.m., were his mom and dad, four siblings and three of their spouses, six other relatives, nine BYU buddies led by NFL punter Lee Johnson, Young's girlfriend at the time, Stephanie Weston, 10 friends, three agents and one reporter. To no one in particular, a depleted Young said: "Is this great or what? I mean, I haven't thrown six touchdown passes in any game in my life. Then I throw six today in the Super Bowl! Unbelievable."

Someone in the crowd said: "Joe who?"

"No, don't do that," Young said. "Don't worry about that. That's the past. Let's talk the future."

What a night. But as Young said, let's talk the future. The prototype quarterback of the next century—after a series of concussions, Young faced possible retirement in 1999 at age 38, still near the top of his game—may well be in the Steve Young mold: tremendously accurate (a 64.5% career completion rate, about eight percentage points higher than the average passer of his day), with machine-like efficiency (his 97.5 passer rating is the best of all time), and running-back mobility. Ris-

Young

in SI's words

Coach George Seifert calls the shots on the field, owner Eddie DeBartolo Jr. coughs up the cash, and president Carmen Policy cuts the deals. But Super Bowl MVP Steve Young is the leader of the 49ers, the man whose spirit and drive have propelled this team to its lofty perch....

When 49er fans chanted "Steve! Steve!" as Young took his buoyant victory lap around Candlestick Park following last month's NFC championship victory over Dallas, it was more than a recognition of the 33-year-old quarterback's rigorous quest to escape Joe Montana's shadow. In their delirious state, the Candlestick fans were merely echoing the sentiment that Young's teammates had acknowledged a month earlier when they selected him as the winner of the Len Eshmont Award—given to the most courageous and inspirational 49er player—for the second time in three years.

After four years as Montana's impatient backup, then three more years of starting duty accompanied by constant questions as to whether the 49ers were his team, Young had answered all the skepticism and led his team to victory. The 49ers, winners of four Super Bowls under Montana's guidance, were on their way to a fifth title, and there was absolutely no doubt as to who had led them there.
—Michael Silver, April 24, 1995

ing stars like Steve McNair and Mark Brunell, with their strong arms and great mobility, come to mind.

Rest assured Young is not so high on this list because of one great night and one good story. He's here because of his multifaceted excellence and will to win, both of which survived stints in the United States Football League and with the woeful Tampa Bay Buccaneers during the first four years of his pro career. He threw passes to pinpoints.

He could not throw a Marino–esque bullet, but his high, arcing spirals found his receivers just the same. He ran as well as any quarterback ever, including Fran Tarkenton and Randall Cunningham. His weaving, bobbing touchdown run to beat Minnesota in the 1988 regular season was picked as the best run ever by NFL Films in 1990. His mastery of a game plan rivaled Montana's.

Above all, though, it was Young's desire that separated him from the pack.

In 1999, when a neurologist told him he'd have to miss a game because of a concussion suffered against Arizona, Steinberg told Young that it was good news, that maybe he'd only miss this one game. His backup, Jeff Garcia, a Canadian Football League refugee, would make his first NFL start in Young's place.

"Good news?" Young said. "That's not good news. I don't want to give Jeff a chance to take my job." That's the way the best quarterbacks of all time think.

<u>8</u> Terry Bradshaw

A tough, fiery leader, he overcame a
rocky early career to guide
Pittsburgh to four Super Bowl titles

Bradshaw led
Pittsburgh to a 21–17
triumph over Dallas in
Super Bowl X (right),
his second title with
the Steelers; he
would lead them to
two more champi-
onships before suc-
cumbing to elbow
injuries and closing
his Hall of Fame
career in 1983 (left).

True story: Terry Bradshaw was a coin flip away from being a Chicago Bear.

Because the Steelers and Bears each finished 1–13 in 1969, commissioner Pete Rozelle had to flip a coin to determine which of the two cellar dwellers would get the first choice in the 1970 draft. The coin toss was scheduled for a New Orleans hotel ballroom during Super Bowl week in 1970. From the stage of the ballroom, Chicago president Ed McCaskey would call the toss for the Bears while Pittsburgh owner Art Rooney sat opposite him, representing the Steelers. Rozelle lofted the 1921 silver dollar into the stuffy ballroom air and McCaskey called heads. The coin plunked onto the cloth-covered table and everyone leaned in to see the result. "Tails," Rozelle called.

"McCaskey, you bum!" hollered a Bears fan from the back of the room. "You couldn't even win a coin toss!"

For a while, though, the Steelers may have regretted winning that flip. Brad-

shaw was slow to emerge as a superstar. In college at Louisiana Tech, he hadn't run a terribly sophisticated offense, relying heavily on his athleticism. The combination of a quiet but dictatorial coach in Chuck Noll and the complexity of the pro game frustrated the immature Bradshaw. "I had an apartment out near the airport in Pittsburgh when I first got there," Bradshaw recalled. "And I remember being so depressed early on after I'd had a bad day of practice, that I'd go back to the apartment and just cry. I was so miserable, and I wasn't really friendly with the other guys. They looked at me like a Bible-toting Li'l Abner."

Bradshaw threw only two more touchdown passes (212) than intercep-

tions in his 14-year career. Only twice did he throw for 3,000 yards in a season, the standard for a great year. "My career wasn't all that hot," he said with surprising modesty after his playing days were over. "I had five good years and one great year. I never had good statistics."

You might find it surprising, then, that he is so high on my list of the best quarterbacks ever. (Even he was surprised when I told him. Pleased, but surprised.) That's the beauty of quarterbacking greatness. Otto Graham threw more interceptions than touchdown passes in the NFL. No one cares how you got the team into the end zone, or into the win column. They only care that you did both. Bradshaw quarter-

Pocket Protectors: Pittsburgh's sturdy offensive line shielded Bradshaw as he led the team to championship seasons in 1978 (above) and '79 (opposite, in a 31–19 win over the Rams), and won back-to-back Super Bowl MVP awards.

backed eight division winners and went 4–0 in Super Bowls.

Further proof that Bradshaw was destined for greatness is his involvement in the most unlikely touchdown pass of all time—the Immaculate Reception—on December 23, 1972, Bradshaw's third year in the league. A desperate, last-second pass that ricocheted off of one player and was plucked out of the air by running back Franco Harris, who took it in for a score, the Immaculate Reception vaulted Pittsburgh past Oakland and into the 1972 AFC championship game. Bradshaw, smashed to the ground by a ferocious Raider pass rush, didn't

see the end of the play. When he heard the immense roar from the Three Rivers Stadium crowd he knew something positive had happened for his team. It was a sound he'd get used to hearing over the next decade.

Yet even that fateful play didn't make Bradshaw the Steelers' full-time starter. He was platooned for much of his first four seasons. After one game, he was leaving a downtown parking garage and the attendant told him, "Boy, you stunk today." Not until midway through the 1974 season did Bradshaw claim the starting job. Pittsburgh reached its first Super Bowl after that season. Bradshaw gained confidence each

Bradshaw

"Very few people can go through life and say they were the very best at what they did. I am one of the people who can say, not that I was the very best, but that *we* were, and that's a privilege."

—Terry Bradshaw

turningpoint

Bristling with talent and athletic ability when he came out of Louisiana Tech in 1970 as the No.-1 draft pick, Terry Bradshaw was notably lacking in one area, familiarity with the complexities of the pro game. "I didn't learn any football in college," Bradshaw once said. "I didn't learn anything about coverages. So I had this whole big adjustment."

The transition period was difficult indeed, and nearly derailed Bradshaw's promising career. He struggled for four years, and didn't win the starting job outright until December 1974, after surviving a three-way battle with former Notre Dame star Terry Hanratty and Tennessee State product Joe Gilliam. "After my fifth year," Bradshaw recalled, "I can't remember ever feeling any pressure of losing my job again. That's a great feeling."

It showed as the young quarterback, whose shakiness was acknowledged even by his teammates, settled down and began to fulfill his immense potential. He led the Steelers to a 32–14 rout of Buffalo in the first round of the playoffs and, in the AFC title game against Oakland, he hit Lynn Swann with a game-winning six-yard touchdown pass in the fourth quarter.

The following week in New Orleans Bradshaw would be fitted for a Super Bowl ring as the Steelers defeated Minnesota 16–6. He would wear three more before decade's end.

THE RECORD

YEAR	TEAM	G	ATT	COMP	COMP%	YDS	TD	INT	RATING
1970	Pitt	13	218	83	38.1	1410	6	24	30.4
1971	Pitt	14	373	203	54.4	2259	13	22	59.7
1972	Pitt	14	308	147	47.7	1887	12	12	64.1
1973	Pitt	10	180	89	49.4	1183	10	15	54.5
1974	Pitt	8	148	67	45.3	785	7	8	55.2
1975	Pitt	14	286	165	57.7	2055	18	9	88.0
1976	Pitt	10	192	92	47.9	1177	10	9	65.4
1977	Pitt	14	314	162	51.6	2523	17	19	71.4
1978	Pitt	16	368	207	56.3	2915	28	20	84.7
1979	Pitt	16	472	259	54.9	3724	26	25	77.0
1980	Pitt	16	424	218	51.4	3339	24	22	75.0
1981	Pitt	14	370	201	54.3	2887	22	14	83.9
1982	Pitt	9	240	127	52.9	1768	17	11	81.4
1983	Pitt	1	8	5	62.5	77	2	0	133.9
TOTAL		168	3901	2025	51.9	27,989	212	210	70.9

Bradshaw

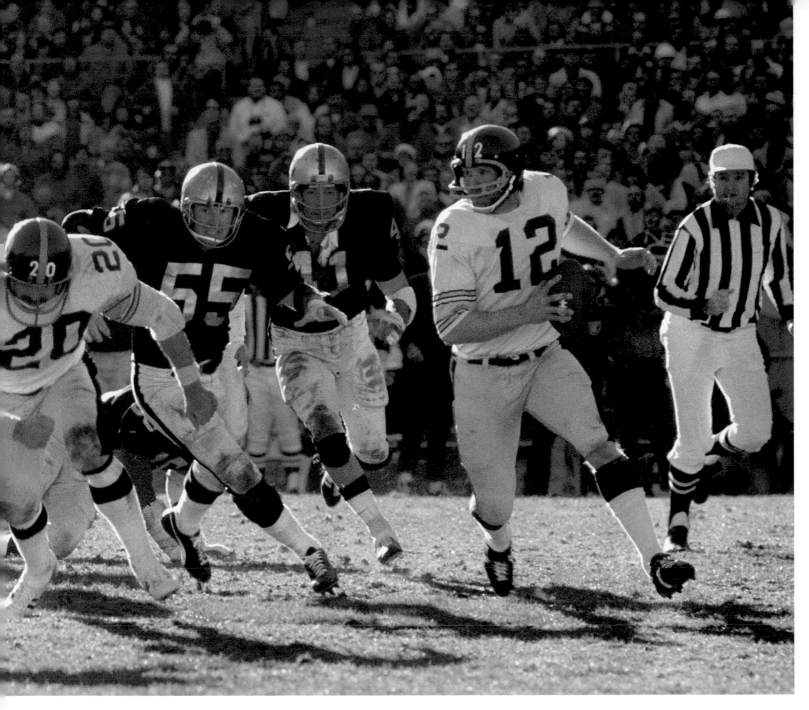

With the great running backs Rocky Bleier (above, 20), a superb blocker, and Franco Harris (opposite, 32), a Hall of Fame runner, in his backfield, Bradshaw (12) knew that he didn't have to do it alone on offense.

week and began a 10-year starting run.

He won two Super Bowl MVP awards, and when he needed to, he willed wins. In Super Bowl X, against Dallas, he threw a touchdown pass to tight end Randy Grossman to tie the game in the first quarter. In the fourth quarter he made the type of play that put him on this list, in this spot. The Dallas pass rush had been heating up in the second half, with Ed (Too Tall) Jones making regular visits to the Steelers backfield. From the Pittsburgh 36, Bradshaw

faded back to pass, and here came the Cowboys again. Spotting wideout Lynn Swann behind the Dallas secondary, Bradshaw launched the ball as he was leveled by two Cowboys, his head thudding hard on the ground. Swann made a balletic catch for a 64-yard touchdown. The Steelers held on to win 21–17.

"Didn't see it," Bradshaw said. "They knocked me unconscious just as the ball was released. But it looked good on film." Like many of the plays this winner made in his Hall-of-Fame career.

9 BrettFavre

Assuming Favre (above, in 1996, and left, handing off to Vince Workman in 1992) can stay healthy and steer clear of alcohol problems, he could have another decade or so of excellence ahead of him.

It's a tricky job, trying to find a place in history for a quarterback while he's still in his prime. A few days before his 30th birthday in 1999, Brett Favre rested on a trainer's table in Green Bay, icing and electronically stimulating his badly swollen right thumb. I told him he was going to rank ninth on the alltime list of great quarterbacks in this book.

"Right ahead of Babe Laufenberg?" he deadpanned.

"Blair Kiel," I said.

He gave a slight smile.

"Where do I send the check?"

The exchange said a lot about Brett Favre. He's mentally quick, very quick, and this trait has served him superbly on the football field. He's also self-effacing and has a good sense of humor, which has made him king of the Packer locker room, before and after Green Bay heroes Mike Holmgren and Reggie White departed.

Favre has achieved all of his considerable feats—the game-winning touchdown passes, the three MVP awards, the one Super Bowl, the durability that yielded the longest starting quarterback streak in the NFL since 1970—before his 30th birthday. That's why he's in my Top 10. The only question that remains is how high he will rise on this list when his career is over. He's healthy, he still has a fine offense and he hungers to be good for a long time, to leave a mark.

"When you're young, you play for money," he said from the trainer's table. "But after you get a lot of money, you're playing to win. When we lost to Detroit a couple weeks ago, I wanted to shoot myself."

If his second decade in the game is anything like his first, there will be lots of plays like the last throw he made in his 20s. It came during Week 3 of the 1999 season. The Packers were playing the Vikings, and trailing 20–16 in the fourth quarter. Green Bay had the ball on fourth-and-one at the Minnesota 23. They had no timeouts and the clock was running.

:18 ... :17 ... :16 ...

"I was tired," Favre said, "as tired as I'd ever been in my life on the field. I started getting sick before the game with this flu, and I was dehydrated, and we're losing. We hadn't done anything all day. So we don't get the first down the play before, the clock's running, and we're just walking to the line. I say, 'Line up!' Everybody's asking for the formation, the play, and I say, 'Just line up!' So they line up, four across, two on one side, two on the other. I'm so dry I'm spitting cotton balls. I give everybody the signal"—he raised both hands and wiggled the index and middle fingers together on each—"which means go or quick stop, depending on the coverage. If they get bumped, they go. If they're given room, they stop. It looks like we got bump-and-run across the board. Then the ball's in my hands. I don't remember saying a word.

"Later, [center] Frankie [Winters] told me [Viking lineman] John Randle

called the snap for me, trying to confuse us. "Somebody yelled 'Set-HUT,' and I got the ball. Then I'm thinking, I don't know if my guys know the situation. If I throw this and they don't know to get out of bounds, game's over. I look at the field, and it is bump-and-run, and I say to myself, 'This is it. Somebody's got to win their battle.' I look to the right, at Bill Schroeder, pump right, keep the safety there, then turn back. Sure

enough, Corey Bradford gets free. I threw it as hard as I could. Corey just got under it and hung on.

"Amazing. We call no play, Minnesota calls our snap count, we win. I'm running around the field like a wild man after that play, then I come over to the bench, bang my head against the bench when I lay down, and John Gray, our doctor, takes my pulse. My heart rate's 210. He says: 'Lucky you

don't have heart problems. You'd be dead.'"

After that game, Favre met coach Ray Rhodes near the door of the Packer locker room. "You gotta stop doing this to me!" Rhodes said, hugging Favre. "Once, fine. But you're gonna give me a heart attack."

Favre's future—assuming he can stay free of alcohol, an acknowledged demon which he has sworn off twice in his career—is a bright one. He could be great

Favre (above, right, and above, versus Denver in 1996) possesses the strength to throw bullets even when off balance and to shed tacklers like a running back.

THE RECORD

YEAR	TEAM	G	ATT	COMP	COMP%	YDS	TD	INT	RATING
1991	Atl	2	5	0	00.0	0	0	2	00.0
1992	GB	15	471	302	64.1	3227	18	13	85.3
1993	GB	16	522	318	60.9	3303	19	24	72.2
1994	GB	16	582	363	62.4	3882	33	14	90.7
1995	GB	16	570	359	63.0	4413	38	13	99.5
1996	GB	16	543	325	59.9	3899	39	13	95.8
1997	GB	16	513	304	59.3	3867	35	16	92.6
1998	GB	16	551	347	63.0	4212	31	23	87.8
TOTAL		113	3757	2318	61.7	26,803	213	118	89.0

Like many of our Top 10 quarterbacks, Favre (above and opposite, versus the Steelers in 1992) is a leader capable of inspiring his teammates to perform above and beyond their own expectations.

well into his 30s. "Thirty's a magic number for a lot of people," Favre said. "Now you know the end is coming somewhere down the road. I think, When will this game leave me? I want to make sure before the end comes I can look back and say I was the best possible quarterback I could be. I don't want to turn 37, say, 'Okay, now I'm as smart as I can be,' and my body won't hold up. So I've changed, both as a player and a person. The Friday night before our first game this year [1999], I'm over here watching film at 10:30 with my brother Scott. I turn to him and say, 'Can you believe we're sitting here, 10:30, Friday night, watching film?' Used to be I was out partying. But I had no desire to be anywhere else."

Good news for the Favre family. Great news for Packer fans, and fans of dramatic football.

turningpoint

Before he was a Super Bowl hero and the league's only three-time Most Valuable Player, he was just Bart Favre. At least that's what the Packers mistakenly called him in one of their press releases during his first year in Green Bay. The error was excusable at the time, especially in a town that pined for the glory days of Bart Starr. The Packers had acquired the 22-year-old Favre from Atlanta to back up Don Majkowski. A second-round pick in 1991, Favre had struggled as a Falcon, playing in only two games as a rookie and completing more passes to the opposing team (2) than to his own (0).

On September 20, 1992, the 0–2 Packers, who had gone 4–12 the previous year, were still looking for coach Mike Holmgren's first career victory as they hosted the unbeaten Cincinnati Bengals. Early in the first quarter the Lambeau faithful groaned as Majkowski left the game with an injured ankle.

Enter Favre. During the next three hours, the young quarterback altered the course of the Packers franchise. Down 17–3 after three quarters, Favre rallied Green Bay with two touchdown passes in the last five minutes. His final pass, a 35-yard touchdown to Kitrick Taylor with 13 seconds left, capped a 92-yard, 54-second drive and gave the Packers a 24–23 win. Favre finished with 289 passing yards. "He did things I didn't even know were in the game plan," said Holmgren. With Favre at the controls, the Packers became winners. Green Bay would finish the season 9–7, its second-best record in 20 years, and a Super Bowl title was only four years away.

"Reporters would ask me where I got my arm. I always thought it was from my father, but now I think I got it from my mother, She got mad at me last summer and threw a pastrami sandwich and hit me on the head. Hard. She really had something on that sandwich."

—Brett Favre,
in 1993

10 RogerStaubach

Despite delaying his pro career by four years to fulfill his military obligation to the Navy, Roger the Dodger led Dallas to four Super Bowls, and two NFL titles

Staubach wasn't yet a full-time starter in 1970 (opposite), but he led Dallas to victory in Super Bowl VI (below) in '72, winning 10 straight after getting the job.

Roger Staubach's father noticed something interesting while watching his son play high school baseball in Cincinnati. "I used to dread the ball being hit to me when the game was tight," he told Roger one day. "You seem to relish it." Roger said yes, he did love it when the ball was hit to him with the game on the line. And he never lost that love of a pressure situation. In the 1970s Staubach specialized in saving the Cowboys' bacon. Fourteen times in the bellbottom decade he rallied Dallas to victory after it had trailed or was tied with fewer than two minutes remaining in the game.

Staubach took a roundabout route to his role of coolest Cowboy at the rodeo. He didn't play quarterback until his senior year in high school. A devout Catholic, he badly wanted to attend Notre Dame, but the Irish had no interest in Staubach as a football player. The Naval Academy did, and Staubach became a Midshipman in 1961. He won the Heisman Trophy in 1963, and Dallas selected him in the 10th round of the '64 draft, knowing that he'd have to miss five seasons but hoping he might have some football left in him when he got out of the Navy prior to the 1969 season.

After spending his final year in the Navy as a supply officer in Vietnam, Staubach latched on with the Cowboys as their third-string quarterback. "I'd kept abreast of the game in the Navy, and played some football and baseball and a lot of basketball," he said. "So I was really no worse off than any rookie coming to the pros from college." Perhaps, but Staubach didn't land the starting job until his third year in Dallas,

Staubach

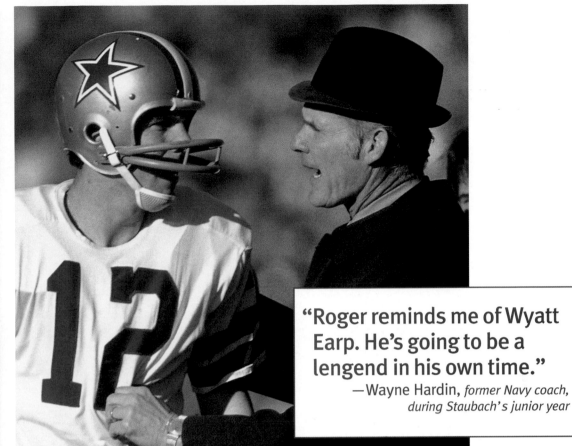

> "Roger reminds me of Wyatt Earp. He's going to be a lengend in his own time."
> —Wayne Hardin, *former Navy coach, during Staubach's junior year*

Ranking Roger: Staubach showed his agility in a 1971 playoff win over Minnesota (left), and his smarts in Super Bowl VI (above), both of which place him 10th on our list.

1971, when he was 29 years old and eight years removed from his last start in a meaningful football game. But what a debut season he had: He went 10–0, was named NFL Player of the Year and took home the Super Bowl MVP trophy as well after the Cowboys steamrolled the Dolphins 24–3 in New Orleans.

His knack for comebacks became evident soon afterward. In a 1972 playoff game against the 49ers, Dallas trailed 28–16 with 90 seconds to play. Staubach hit Billy Parks for a 20-yard touchdown strike and after the Cowboys recovered the ensuing onside kick, he put them back in the end zone in three plays, the last a 10-yard touchdown pass to Ron Sellers. Dallas 30, San Francisco 28. He threw a 50-yard pass to Drew Pearson in the waning seconds to beat Minnesota in a frigid playoff game in Minneapolis in 1975.

A month before his 36th birthday Staubach led Dallas to its second Super Bowl win, a 27–10 triumph over Denver in Supe XII. The following year, with Dallas trailing Pittsburgh 35–17 with three minutes to play in Super Bowl XIII, Staubach nearly made another spectacular comeback. He hit Billy Joe DuPree and Butch Johnson with touchdown passes to pull Dallas to within four. If the Cowboys had recovered another onside kick, who

Staubach could go deep, as Miami found out in 1978 (above), and he had an uncanny knack for the dramatic comeback, which he nearly pulled off in Super Bowl X (opposite) against Pittsburgh, throwing for a late score before being intercepted in the end zone as time ran out in the Steelers' 21–17 win.

knows? There were 22 seconds left for Roger to operate. As it happened, the Steelers held on, 35–31. In his last regular-season game, at age 37, Staubach threw two touchdown passes in the final 2½ minutes to beat the archrival Washington Redskins.

Were it not for a series of concussions in the NFL and a New York neurosurgeon's recommendation that he quit in 1980, Staubach might have played two or three more years. In the fall of 1999, though, he had no regrets. "I had a great career," he said, "and I've

never thought for a moment I should have stayed in, even though I physically felt fine."

Along the way, Staubach became the anti-*North Dallas Forty* leader of America's Team, a straight arrow with five children. He was a hero to every kid in Texas. To every teammate, too, apparently. "There's nobody I ever met who was a better leader," said Randy White, the Hall of Fame defensive tackle who played with Staubach from 1975 to 1979. "Here's a story I'll never forget: My rookie year, I walk into a

locker room with Roger, Ed Jones, Harvey Martin, Preston Pearson—all the great players from that great Cowboy era. And one of the first games, I remember Roger coming to me in the locker room before we went out, putting his arm around me, shaking my hand and saying: 'Randy, we really need you to play great today to win. Let's go get 'em.' Me, just out of college. And Roger says that. Wow. You think after Roger Staubach says that to me I don't want to go out and run through a wall for him?"

THE RECORD

YEAR	TEAM	G	ATT	COMP	COMP%	YDS	TD	INT	RATING
1969	Dall	6	47	23	48.9	421	1	2	69.5
1970	Dall	8	82	44	53.7	542	2	8	42.9
1971	Dall	13	211	126	59.7	1882	15	4	104.8
1972	Dall	4	20	9	45.0	98	0	2	20.4
1973	Dall	14	286	179	62.6	2428	23	15	94.6
1974	Dall	14	360	190	52.8	2552	11	15	68.4
1975	Dall	13	348	198	56.9	2666	17	16	78.5
1976	Dall	14	369	208	56.4	2715	14	11	79.9
1977	Dall	14	361	210	58.2	2620	18	9	87.0
1978	Dall	15	413	231	55.9	3190	25	16	84.9
1979	Dall	16	461	267	57.9	3586	27	11	92.3
TOTAL		131	2958	1685	57.0	22,700	153	109	83.4

turning**point**

If Chris Weinke, the 1999 Florida State Seminoles' starting quarterback who began his college career as a 25-year-old, decided to leave Tallahassee for the NFL after his junior year, he would enter training camp as Roger Staubach did in 1969: as a 27-year-old rookie. But Weinke would have a leg up on Roger the Dodger since he would be fresh from a nationally contending college program; Staubach came to the Cowboys after four years in the Navy, nearly half a decade out of shoulder pads. Sure, he won the Heisman Trophy in 1963, but how sharp would he be in '69?

Always a quick study, Staubach made the team and battled for playing time with the incumbent, Craig Morton. In 1971 opportunity came knocking, and Staubach sprang for the door. The Cowboys were the defending NFC champs that year, but they lost three of their first seven games. After the third loss, a disheartening 23–19 decision to lowly Chicago, Dallas coach Tom Landry handed the reins over to Staubach. The Cowboys won their first game with Staubach as the starter, and didn't lose again, finishing atop the NFC East at 11–3. They dispatched Minnesota and San Francisco in the playoffs to advance to Super Bowl VI against the Dolphins.

As Dallas's legendary Doomsday Defense shut down the vaunted Miami running game of Larry Csonka and Jim Kiick, Staubach was coolly efficient, hitting Lance Alworth for seven yards and a touchdown in the second quarter, and Mike Ditka for the same in the fourth. He completed 12 of his 19 passes on the day, and was named the game's MVP. The 29-year-old had completed the first step in his journey to Canton.

11-20: They Also Starred

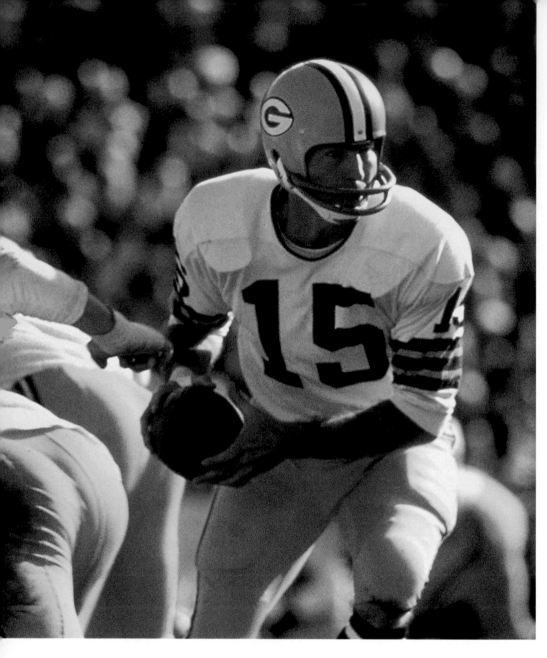

11-20: They also starred

1939 to '50) won four championships in his 12 seasons, and he spearheaded the first T formation to be used extensively in the NFL. The T consisted of a quarterback and two running backs in the backfield, and ushered in the era of the forward pass as an offensive staple in the NFL.

Joe Namath, at No. 12, is here for symbolism (he was the counterculture quarterback) and for his brashness (he boldly predicted and then helped carry out one of the biggest upsets in football history, the Jets' win over the Colts in Super Bowl III). He was also a superb football player. Starr comes in at No. 13 almost in spite of himself. In his on- and off-field demeanor Starr was an anti-star: quiet, unassuming, never flashy. But he won 78% of his starts in an eight-year run of greatness that brought five championships to Green Bay, a.k.a. Titletown.

Then comes Aikman, the three-time champ who is so accurate that his former offensive coordinator, Norv Turner, remembers practices during which, "I wouldn't see the ball hit the ground. His accuracy in games and during the week is the best I've ever seen."

But here's why I've put Starr and Aikman where they are: The Cowboys of the early 1990s, much like the Packers of the '60s, were like a symphony—several dominant players, many superb role players, and in Dallas's case, blinding overall team speed. The league had never seen a team as fast as those Cowboys. When Jimmy Johnson took the Dallas job in 1989, coaches snickered at all the undersized defensive players with track-star speed he seemed to favor, but after Dallas won three Super Bowls, those

Now it gets interesting. Now my method gets overtaken by football madness. I began the book by saying that championships are paramount, yet ranked Bart Starr and Troy Aikman, who won five and three of them, respectively, behind a bunch of players who won fewer titles.

Enter the human element. I can't help it. I think Starr had the best supporting cast—players and coaches combined—in NFL history, even better

than the Browns in their heyday or the Niners that surrounded Joe Montana in the huddle. As for Aikman, his is the era I've watched and covered. I think Montana, John Elway, Dan Marino, Steve Young and Brett Favre are better quarterbacks than Aikman. I could be persuaded otherwise about Favre, but about none of the others.

But we'll come back to that. Let's start at the beginning of our second tier of greats. Sid Luckman (Chicago Bears,

Leon Lett, cornerbacks Darren Woodson and later Deion Sanders, the list goes on.

So yes, I rank Aikman and Starr behind Favre and Young and Elway. I also rank them ahead of Bobby Layne, Sonny Jurgensen and Fran Tarkenton.

Tarkenton is my No. 15. He never won much, but he left the game in 1978 with every quarterback record there was, and they stood until Marino came along. I had a hard time making the call between Nos. 16 and 17, Jurgensen and Dan Fouts, who shared the unfortunate distinction of being Hall of Famers who never won championships. They were the NFL's mad bombers from the Eisenhower administration through the Reagan years, spanning 31 seasons of NFL history.

After Fouts I have Layne, who led the Lions to three championships in the 1950s, and he makes it with a lampshade over his helmet. He was the greatest Lion ever—until Barry Sanders came along—and also Detroit's hardest partier.

Jim Kelly made four Super Bowls orchestrating a quick-hitting Buffalo offense. He's No. 19. Phil Simms, my upset pick at 20, is here because he helped lead two fairly different Giants team to titles. He never hesitated to adjust his role so his team could do whatever was necessary to win. And his Super Bowl XXI performance was the best ever.

So there's my Top 20, selected partly by a game plan and partly by gut-feeling—call it Monday-morning quarterbacking.

coaches stopped laughing, and started imitating.

To support Starr in Green Bay, the Packers fielded such Hall of Famers as running backs Jim Taylor and Paul Hornung, tackle Forrest Gregg and fearsome linebacker Ray Nitschke. They also had the great Lombardi on the sidelines, who would not permit them to lose, and they owned the 1960s, appearing in six championship games.

The Cowboys won Super Bowls after the 1992, '93 and '95 seasons. Emmitt Smith won the rushing title each of those years—by an amazing 273 yards in '95. Physical wideout Michael Irvin finished seventh, third and fifth in the league in receiving in those years. The offensive line was massive and experienced. The defense finished fifth, second and third in points allowed in the championship seasons.

None of this is meant to demean the great play of Aikman. It's meant to put him in historical context. From 1980 to 2000, no team—not even San Francisco—had as many dominant players as Dallas had to complement Aikman: offensive linemen Erik Williams and Larry Allen, the great blocking back Daryl Johnston, tight end Jay Novacek, defensive lineman

11 SidLuckman

In the 1940s, the Chicago Bears star made quarterback the glamour position

The revolutionary Luckman (left, in 1948) was all over the field in the 1943 title game against Washington (below), rushing for 64 yards and passing for five touchdowns in the Bears' 41–21 victory.

The acquisition of Sid Luckman by Chicago Bears owner, coach and founder George Halas is a landmark event in the evolution of the quarterback position in the NFL. And, appropriately enough, the player whose transfer hatched the deal was named Eggs. Eggs Manske.

Halas traded the hardboiled Manske, who was a pretty good defensive lineman for the Bears in 1938, to Pittsburgh, which was the worst team in the league. Papa Bear had scouted Luckman at Columbia in a driving rain in 1938 and thought him an absolute magician with the football. Halas had to have Luckman. So he offered Manske and a lesser player to Pittsburgh for the rights to the Steelers' No. 2 pick in the draft. Pittsburgh agreed.

The NFL Draft wasn't a very big deal in those days, so Luckman found out about his selection in a New York newspaper. "I'd never been further west than

Buffalo," he said later in life. "I thought Chicago was where cowboys were still around. But the Bears offered me a contract for $5,000. George Halas told me: 'You and Jesus Christ are the only two I would ever pay $5,000.' That was pretty big money then, and so I went."

Quarterbacks, also called tailbacks in those days, ran or ran the option most of the time, and passed only occasionally. It wasn't easy to pass, because the ball was fatter and less streamlined than it is today, and harder to grip. But the Bears were determined to build a passing offense around Luckman. With an infusion of brainpower from renowned college coach Clark Shaughnessy, Halas instituted a new T Formation for the Bears when Luckman came on board.

The T was designed to spread the field so that defenses wouldn't bunch toward the line of scrimmage. The Bears

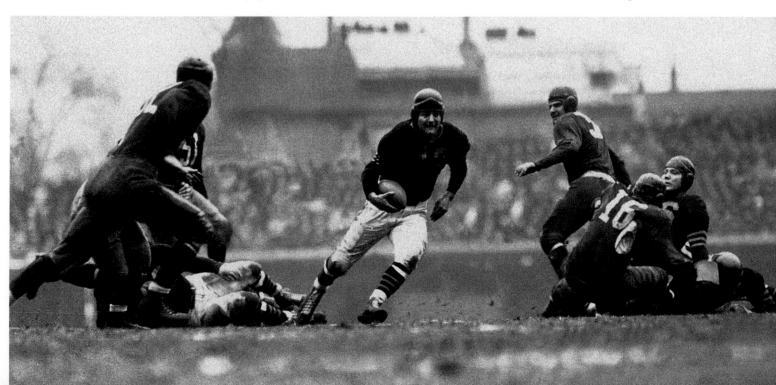

THE RECORD

YEAR	TEAM	G	ATT	COMP	COMP%	YDS	TD	INT	RATING
1939	ChiB	11	51	23	45.1	636	5	4	91.6
1940	ChiB	11	105	48	45.7	941	4	9	54.5
1941	ChiB	11	119	68	57.1	1181	9	6	95.3
1942	ChiB	11	105	57	54.3	1024	10	13	80.1
1943	ChiD	10	202	110	54.5	2194	28	12	107.5
1944	ChiB	7	143	71	49.7	1018	11	12	63.8
1945	ChiB	10	217	117	53.9	1727	14	10	82.5
1946	ChiB	11	229	110	48.0	1826	17	16	71.0
1947	ChiB	12	323	176	54.5	2712	24	31	67.7
1948	ChiB	12	163	89	54.6	1047	13	14	65.1
1949	ChiB	11	50	22	44.0	200	1	3	37.1
1950	ChiB	11	37	13	35.1	180	1	2	38.1
TOTAL		128	1744	904	51.8	14,686	137	132	75.0

Luckman (left, in 1940, and above, in '48) became the prototype for the modern quarterback, able to keep defenses honest with both the pass and the run; football would never be the same.

would often put a man in motion before the snap, to further challenge the defense. In 1940, Halas gave Luckman the keys to this new machine full-time, with the freedom to call his own plays.

The Bears won it all that year, finishing the season with an 11-touchdown onslaught as they shellacked Washington 73–0 in the NFL championship game, still the worst rout in league history. The Bear juggernaut was so impressive that when Washington's Hall of Fame quarterback Sammy Baugh was asked after

the game what he thought the final score might have been had the Skins managed to score on a promising early drive that would have tied the game 7–7, he said, "Seventy-three to seven."

That season did it. After 20 years of domination by the run, the name of the game was passing, and the quarterback was the main man. From the 1940s onward, in the pros and in college (Shaughnessy took the formation to Stanford in 1940, winning the Rose Bowl with it in his first year), the T for-

mation held sway, and befuddled defenses. Defenders couldn't load up against the run anymore. They had to respect the pass. And so was born the modern chess match of offensive coordinator-versus-defensive coordinator that we see every week in the NFL.

"With Sid," Halas once said, "we created a new type of football player—the T quarterback. Newspapers switched their attention from the star runner to the quarterback. It marked a new era for the game. Colleges used Luckman as their

Luckman

model in molding quarterbacks. In Sid's 12 years with the Bears, football was completely revolutionized."

A wiry, six-foot, 190-pounder, Luckman had a surprisingly strong arm, a great touch and tremendous accuracy. You watch NFL Films footage of the guy, and you see a skinny player who easily evaded the rush and threw that fat football farther than it seemed he had a right to. In the 73–0 blitzkrieg of Washington, Luckman ran and passed for touchdowns in the first half, then sat back and watched the carnage. In 1943 he threw seven touchdown passes in the Bears' 56–7 rout of the Giants, and then passed for five more, including a 66-yard strike to Dante Magnani, in the championship game as the Bears romped over Washington again, 41–21.

Luckman even went to colleges in the offseason—Notre Dame and Columbia, among others—free of charge to teach the passing game. With all due respect to Green Bay coach and passing pioneer Curly Lambeau, who designed a passing attack around receiver Don Hutson in the late 1930s, it's fair to say that Luckman is the man who made the passing game what it is today.

And his legacy runs deeper. For 14 years after he retired, Luckman was a part-time assistant to Halas, tutoring quarterbacks and offensive assistant coaches in the art of the pass. He never took a cent in salary. "I can never repay the Bears for making my life a more enchanting life," he said.

Turned out Sid Luckman led the burgeoning NFL in two things: passing and class.

Luckman came a long way from his days as a tailback at Columbia (opposite) to his status as pro football's best quarterback (above, left, celebrating the 1946 championship with George McAfee, middle, and Ray McLean, right).

Luckman

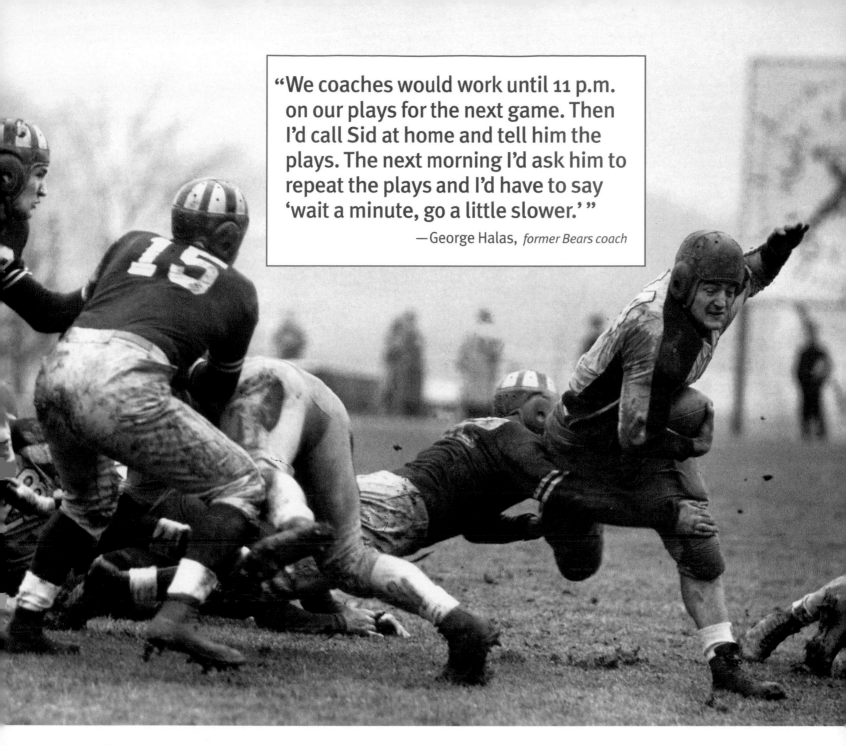

"We coaches would work until 11 p.m. on our plays for the next game. Then I'd call Sid at home and tell him the plays. The next morning I'd ask him to repeat the plays and I'd have to say 'wait a minute, go a little slower.'"

—George Halas, *former Bears coach*

inSI'swords

When Sid Luckman died in July, at 81, the last originator of the oldest offensive formation still in use was gone. The T with a man in motion was the brain work of a coaching triumvirate of George Halas, Clark Shaughnessy and Ralph Jones, and Luckman, a 22-year-old Chicago Bears rookie out of Columbia, was the man chosen to implement it on the field. That was in 1939, and the basic set remains.

"I'd been a single-wing tailback," Luckman said when I visited him at his Fort Lauderdale suburban apartment in May. "You're set deep, the ball comes to you, and you either pass, run or spin. When I came to the Bears, we worked for hours on my spinning, on hiding the ball, only this time it was as a T quarterback. They brought in the old Bears quarterback, Carl Brumbaugh, to work with me. We spent endless time just going over my footwork, faking, spinning, setting up as fast as I could, running to my left and throwing right, days and days of it."

Luckman seemed frail as we talked. All the charm that I remembered from the dozen or so times I had interviewed him through the years was there, but he'd occasionally stop to gather himself, to get things just right. Seated with him at a table heaped with charts and memorabilia and the scrapbooks of a lifetime in the game, I felt as if I were listening to Orville Wright describing the origins of the flying machine.

—Paul Zimmerman, August 17,1998

<u>12</u> JoeNamath

Football's first bonus baby, the brash kid out of Alabama helped pull off the game's greatest upset

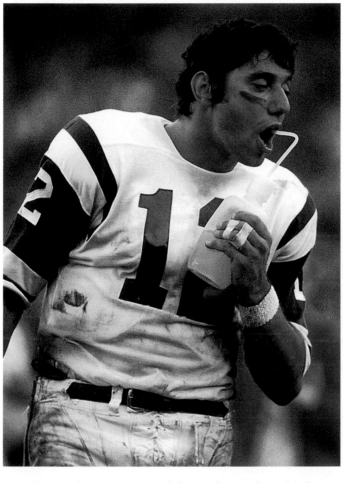

Namath took a moment to cool off in Super Bowl III (right), during which he was definitely hot, completing 17 of 28 passes to lead the underdog Jets in a stunner over Baltimore; the Jets haven't won a title since, including in 1974 (left) when they slogged to a 7–7 record.

Too often when the subject of Joe Namath comes up, the memory of one day in Miami—January 12, 1969—is the only topic that gets discussed. During the week leading up to Super Bowl III, Namath had a few drinks one night at a banquet and stood up and guaranteed a Jets victory on Sunday.

The rag-tag Jets of the AFL were 18-point underdogs to the mighty Colts of the NFL. Yet Namath believed they could win, or he said he did, any-

way. And he made good on his boast, leading the Jets to a 16–7 win over Baltimore. The yellowing NFL Films clip of Namath jogging off the field after the game with his right index finger in the air is one of the most memorable, goose-bump-inducing sequences in league lore.

But we should remember Namath for other reasons also. For one, he saved the American Football League in 1965 when he spurned the NFL and signed a

contract with the upstart Jets, bagging a handsome $437,000. He was one of the first ultra-famous, look-at-me athletes, doing commercials for everything from pantyhose to lounge chairs to popcorn poppers to razors. He also succeeded in the rough-and-tumble world of pro football with the worst pair of knees a star ever had. He was the first quarterback to throw for 4,000 yards in one season, which he did in 1967. He was New York's most eligible bachelor, and Joe Cool at the same time, maybe the last athlete who admitted to staying out till 4 a.m. consistently and being proud of it. "I don't like to date so much as I like to kind of, you know, run into somethin', man," he once said. Perhaps not the legacy he would like, in retrospect. But that was Broadway Joe.

Sometimes the playboy legend of Namath obscures his brilliance and his courage. Take the game before Super Bowl III, the 1968 AFL championship game at Shea Stadium against the Oakland Raiders. In the first quarter

Namath resprained his throwing thumb. In the second quarter Namath got sandwiched by two Raiders, severely dislocating his left ring finger. When he stood up his finger was jutting out at a right angle from his hand. Namath went to trainer Jeff Snedeker and held out his hand. "It's going to hurt, Joe," Snedeker said. "It already hurts," Namath said. The trainer yanked the finger quickly and deftly, snapping it back into place. Namath didn't miss a play.

Just before halftime the Raiders' Ike Lassiter steamed around one end and (not so) Gentle Ben Davidson came around the other as Namath fired an incompletion. Lassiter and Davidson barreled into Namath simultaneously, crushing him to

the frozen turf. Today, Namath would be out for the game—and maybe the next one, with good reason—with a concussion. Back then, he stood up and made it to the locker room for the intermission, mostly under his own power.

At halftime the team doctor told coach Weeb Ewbank to get his backup ready, but Namath insisted on continuing. On the first play of the third quarter he was still woozy, stumbling back from center and falling for a four-yard loss.

Having gathered himself later in the

quarter, he threw a 20-yard touchdown pass to tight end Pete Lammons; Jets, 20–13. Oakland kicked a field goal and scored a touchdown to go up 23–20. Driving his team against a stiff crosswind, Namath took the Jets to the Raider six-yard line with just under eight minutes left. Back to pass on first down, he looked for halfback Bill Mathis. Covered. He looked for wideout George Sauer. Covered. He looked for Lammons. Covered. He looked for his fourth and final option, Don Maynard, who was diago-

> ## "Mainly we wanted to see how good he was. He really didn't throw the ball that damn well for a long time. Now we know how good he is—the best."
> —Curley Johnson, *former Jets punter on Namath's first season in the pros*

As a second-year pro in 1966, Namath (right) helped boost the Jets from 5-8-1 the previous season to 6-6-2; a decade later (left) he still had his powerful throwing arm, but his knees had deteriorated badly, forcing him to retire after the 1977 season.

THE RECORD

YEAR	TEAM	G	ATT	COMP	COMP%	YDS	TD	INT	RATING
1965	NYJ	13	340	164	48.2	2220	18	15	68.8
1966	NYJ	14	471	232	49.3	3379	19	27	62.6
1967	NYJ	14	491	251	52.5	4007	26	28	73.8
1968	NYJ	14	380	187	49.2	3147	15	17	72.1
1969	NYJ	14	361	185	51.2	2734	19	17	74.3
1970	NYJ	5	179	90	50.3	1259	5	12	54.7
1971	NYJ	4	59	28	47.5	537	5	6	68.2
1972	NYJ	13	324	162	50.0	2816	19	21	72.5
1973	NYJ	6	133	68	51.1	966	5	6	68.7
1974	NYJ	14	361	191	52.9	2616	20	22	69.4
1975	NYJ	14	326	157	48.2	2286	15	28	51.0
1976	NYJ	11	230	114	49.6	1090	4	16	39.9
1977	LARm	4	107	50	46.7	606	3	5	54.5
TOTAL		140	3762	1886	50.1	27,663	173	220	65.5

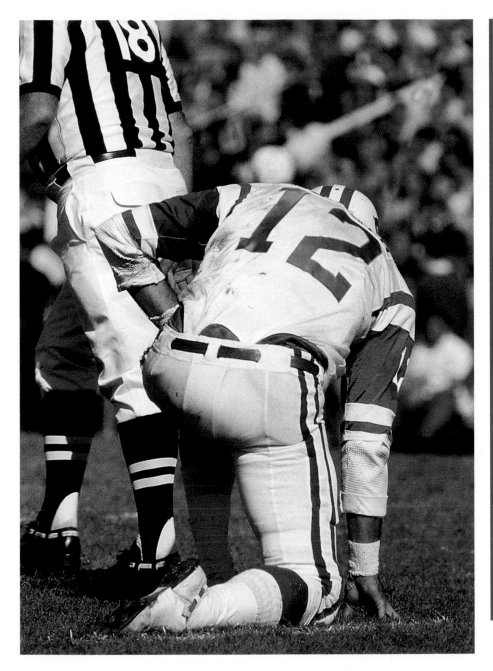

Stoop-shouldered and sinisterly handsome, he slouches against the wall of the saloon, a filter cigarette in his teeth, collar open, perfectly happy and self-assured, gazing through the uneven darkness to sort out the winners from the losers. As the girls come by wearing their miniskirts, net stockings, big false eyelashes, long pressed hair and soulless expressions, he grins approvingly and says, "Hey, hold it, man—foxes." It is Joe Willie Namath at play. Relaxing. Nighttiming. The boss mover studying the defensive tendencies of New York's off-duty secretaries, stewardesses, dancers, nurses, Playboy bunnies, actresses, shopgirls—all of the people who make life stimulating for a bachelor who can throw one of the best passes in pro football. He poses a question for us all: Would you rather be young, single, rich, famous, talented and happy—or president?...

Namath is unlike all of the super sports celebrities who came before him in New York—Babe Ruth, Joe DiMaggio and Sugar Ray Robinson, to name three of the more obvious. They were grown men when they achieved the status he now enjoys. Might've even worn hats. They were less hip to their times and more or less aloof from the crowd. Joe thrusts himself into the middle of it. Their fame came more slowly—with years of earning it. Joe Willie Namath was a happening.
—Dan Jenkins, October 17, 1966

The Broncos may have put him on his back (left), and he occasionally had to struggle to get back up (right), but Joe never got the willies during that magical championship season of 1968.

nally across the field from Namath. And open. Sort of. Namath winged a sidearm shot through the wind, and Maynard made a sliding catch. Touchdown.

Plays like that showed the true wonder of Joe Namath—the arm and the guts and guile and the will to win that too few people remember today. Early in his career, someone asked the bonus baby, the high-living playboy and franchise savior how he'd like to be remembered after he left the game. "I'd like to

be known as a good quarterback, not a rich one," he said, and he wasn't kidding.

No one endures the pain Namath did unless they have an insatiable desire to compete and win. Sometimes that part of his character got masked by his star charisma. "He was the biggest thing in New York since Babe Ruth," said former Patriots owner Billy Sullivan. It's fine if you remember him for his off-the-field legend. Just don't forget to give him some credit for being a damn good player too.

Namath

13 BartStarr

The Starr Report: The ultimate team player, the Green Bay quarterback ranks 13th on our list of the alltime greats for his quiet excellence as he guided the Packers to the first two Super Bowl titles, after the 1966 and '67 seasons (left, and right, respectively).

He never threw 300 passes in a season. He never threw for 3,000 yards. He never said, "Look at me." But Bart Starr was the perfect quarterback for a near-perfect team.

"Bart Starr stands for what the game of football stands for—courage, stamina, coordinated efficiency," his mentor, Vince Lombardi, once said. "You instill desire by creating a superlative example. The noblest form of leadership is by example, and that is what Bart Starr is all about."

Lombardi needed a stolid, stoic leader for his team, a man who would never question the coach, who would run the scheme that was called, and who didn't mind going with the program at a time when it was becoming fashionable to rebel. In short, a man who would be the ultimate team player.

Bart Starr was that man, but he was also one of the best long-shot stories in the NFL. After the Packers traded their starting quarterback, Tobin

Rote, to Detroit in 1957, and gave up on onetime prospect Jim Capuzzi the same year, Starr split time with quarterback Babe Parilli for two years.

That's not unusual for a 17th-round draft pick, which is what Starr was out of Alabama in 1956. "It's obvious they thought I was not going to stay very long," Starr said later in his life. "In our first photo session, they gave me number 42. In fact, I wore that number on my first football card."

Lombardi, who came on board in '59, was big on ball-control. Starr was lousy throwing the deep ball, but he was an excellent short passer, who rarely made mistakes. The match was serendipitous.

After he retired, Starr said that a partnership between Rote and Lombardi would have produced as many championships as he and Lombardi won.

Maybe, but Starr was undeniably Lombardi's perfect quarterback. The epic football game on New Year's Eve 1967 proved that. Chilly that day. Minus-46 degrees with the wind chill, to be exact. Dallas was in Green Bay to play for the NFL championship—the winner would meet the the American Football League champion in Super Bowl II. In the morning before the game Cowboys tackle Bob Lilly threw a cup of water against the window in his hotel room, and the water froze before it could run down the window pane.

The Cowboys, though, had no trouble coping with the cold once the game started. With just under five minutes left, they had a 17–14 lead. And Green Bay, which hadn't done much with the ball on offense since the second quarter, was one failed drive away from a long, cold winter. They'd already won four league titles. Subconsciously, maybe there would be a little something creeping into the back of their minds. Something like: Well, we had a great run. This is a day fit for neither man nor Packer. Let's give it the old college try and go home to get warm.

Starr's teammates said later that they knew they'd drive downfield when they saw the fire in their quarterback's eyes in the huddle. With a short pass to Donnie Anderson and an eight-yard run by Chuck Mercein—the glory days of Paul Hornung and Jim Taylor were over by then—Starr began the

THE RECORD

YEAR	TEAM	G	ATT	COMP	COMP%	YDS	TD	INT	RATING
1956	GB	9	44	24	54.5	325	2	3	65.1
1957	GB	12	215	117	54.4	1489	8	10	69.3
1958	GB	12	157	78	49.7	875	3	12	41.2
1959	GB	12	134	70	52.2	972	6	7	69.0
1960	GB	12	172	98	57.0	1358	4	8	70.8
1961	GB	14	295	172	58.3	2418	16	16	80.3
1962	GB	14	285	178	62.5	2438	12	9	90.7
1963	GB	13	244	132	54.1	1855	15	10	82.3
1964	GB	14	272	163	59.9	2144	15	4	97.1
1965	GB	14	251	140	55.8	2055	16	9	89.0
1966	GB	14	251	156	62.2	2257	14	3	105.0
1967	GB	14	210	115	54.8	1823	9	17	64.4
1968	GB	12	171	109	63.7	1617	15	8	104.3
1969	GB	12	148	92	62.2	1161	9	6	89.9
1970	GB	14	255	140	54.9	1645	8	13	63.9
1971	GB	4	45	24	53.3	286	0	3	45.2
TOTAL		196	3149	1808	57.4	24,718	152	138	80.5

Starr and the Packers began their ascendancy in 1960 (above), when they lost to the Eagles in the NFL title game; they would appear in five more title tilts in the '60s, including Super Bowl I after the '66 season (opposite), and win them all.

> "Honey, we're going to start winning again."
> —Bart Starr, *to his wife, Cherry, after Vince Lombardi became the Packers' coach*

Packer march from the Green Bay 32. It was more of the same as he methodically marched the Pack downfield. With 16 seconds left in the game, Green Bay had the ball on the Dallas one. Starr went to the sidelines.

Common sense told Lombardi he should kick the field goal and take his chances in overtime. But he decided that the day was so ferociously cold he didn't want his team—and the fans, he later joked—to be outside for any longer than they had to be. "I can sneak the ball in," Starr told Lombardi. Okay, said Lombardi, but Starr decided to let his teammates think the play would be a handoff to Mercein. "I thought I was getting the ball," said the running back. When he got to the line, Starr saw Lilly pawing at the ground, trying to get traction. He saw his own linemen getting decent traction on their side of the field. He felt the ground beneath his feet, and was sure he could get some

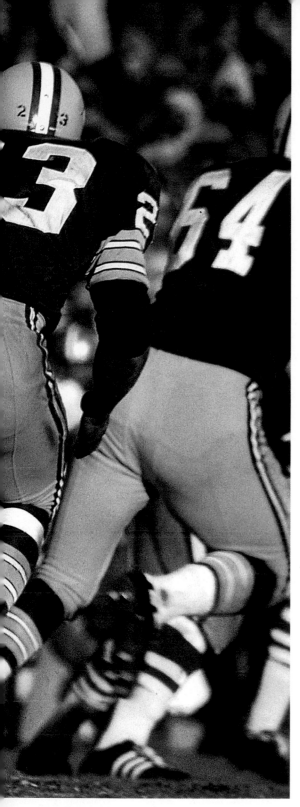

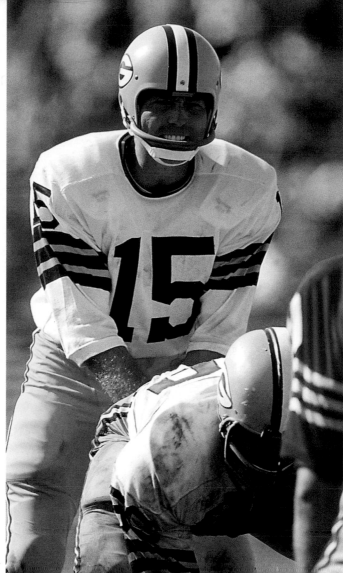

The weather in San Francisco in 1966 (left) was considerably more hospitable to Starr and the Packers than it was the following year during the 1967 NFL title game (opposite), a.k.a. the "Ice Bowl"

footing. Then he took the snap, burrowed in behind guard Jerry Kramer, and didn't stop until the the ball was laying on the ground, in his hands, just beyond the goal line.

Starr knew what he was doing. He always did. He was quiet, but he knew how to get what he wanted.

supportingcast

The career of Bart Starr and the fortunes of the Green Bay Packers took a dramatic turn when newly-hired coach Vince Lombardi told the team in 1959, "I've never been associated with a losing team. I don't intend to start now."

Lombardi had starred at Fordham, where he was one of the legendary Seven Blocks of Granite. As an offensive assistant coach, he helped turn the New York Giants into champions during the 1950s. But the Packers came to him without a winning season since 1947.

The transformation was almost immediate. Lombardi installed Starr as his starting QB in 1959, and the team won seven of its 12 games. His obsessive emphasis on execution, fundamentals, and teamwork ushered in a decade of unprecedented dominance that began when Green Bay won the Western Conference in 1960.

Lombardi's teams could beat you however you liked: with the run, the pass, by a high score, or a low one. His Packer rosters read like a Hall of Fame roll-call: Paul Hornung, Ray Nitschke, Jim Taylor, Herb Adderly, Forrest Gregg, Willie Davis and Willie Wood. In 1961, the Pack blanked the Giants 37–0 in the NFL title game. Four NFL championships and two Super Bowls later, Green Bay was dubbed Titletown and the name Lombardi had became synonymous with winning. Indeed, after the great coach lost his battle with cancer in 1970, the Super Bowl trophy was named in his honor.

Since then, there have been coaches who have won more games and more Super Bowls than Lombardi, but no coach has left a greater imprint on the sport.

14 Troy Aikman

One of the most accurate passers ever, he led Dallas to three Super Bowl titles, no mean feat in the era of free agency

Aikman and Dallas (opposite and below) fell short of the Super Bowl in '94, losing to San Francisco in the NFC title game, but they returned to glory after the '95 season.

In January 1996, after the Dallas Cowboys won their third Super Bowl of the 1990s, Troy Aikman invited me to stop by his postgame party at the team hotel. This was in Arizona, after Dallas beat the Steelers 27–17. I took him up on his offer.

A country band played in a hotel restaurant that gave the appearance of being carved out of a huge rock. The party wasn't very loud. In fact, that's what I remember most about that night. Surrounded by 150 friends and family, this was about as subdued a winners' party for anything—Super Bowl, Little League baseball, my daughter's soccer team—as I'd ever seen. People smiled, and there was some good ol' boy back-slapping, and a good bit of drinking, and maybe things got crazy by two or three in the morning. But from what I saw, the party was fairly serene, composed, just like Aikman.

As I flew home the day after the Super Bowl, I compared the Aikman affair to the Dom Perignon–guzzling, high-decibel party that Dallas coach Barry Switzer had *two nights before* the game in his suite, and I thought, Who's the responsible one here—Coach Switzer or his 29-year-old quarterback?

After Jimmy Johnson's stormy but effective two-Super Bowl reign atop the Cowboys, owner Jerry Jones made the decision (questionable at the time, idiotic in hindsight) to hire Barry Switzer as Johnson's replacement. The Cowboys lost in the playoffs in Switzer's first year. They did win the aforementioned Super Bowl in his second, but they crashed and burned in Switzer's final two seasons, 1996 and '97. As Rome burned, Jones assigned Aikman a role that remains singular among NFL

players. Aikman pooh-poohs it, but his word is gold with the owner, and when he whispers something to Jones, it almost always gets done.

And although there were many Best Supporting Actors in the Dallas mini-dynasty, and it was by far the most well-rounded team of the '90s, Aikman was always the top dog. "I attribute my success to him," receiver Michael Irvin said in 1996. "I've never seen anybody throw a better ball. The greatest things I've done, the greatest times—Troy is 100% responsible, and even then I'm understating it." After the third Super Bowl Jones said, "We all have ridden Troy's coattails."

Aikman is a classic drop-back quarterback with drop-dead perfect mechanics and the kind of accuracy coaches see in their dreams. In his three championship seasons, he threw more interceptions than touchdowns in only nine of 55 games. He completed at least 50% of his passes in all but three of those 55 games. Think of it. On any given Sunday, one-third of the starting quarterbacks will have lousy days. Aikman might have had four or five lousy days in three years. He has the kind of

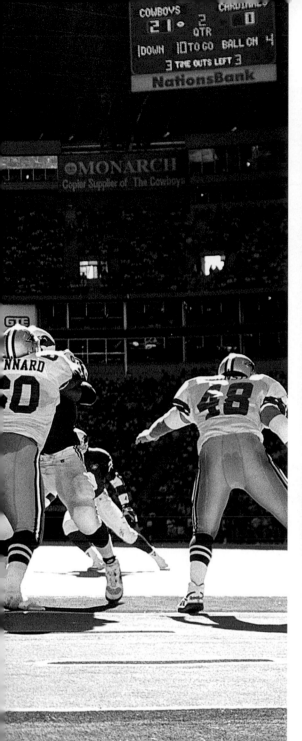

Air Troy: Against the Cardinals in 1994 (left, and above, right) Aikman threw early and often as Dallas romped 38–3 en route to a third straight NFC East crown.

"Nobody but Troy says anything in that huddle. He has their respect.... In Troy's huddle, everyone's there looking at Troy. That says something. If Troy can get that kind of respect from Michael Irvin and Emmitt Smith, you know right away that it's his team."

—Bill Bates, *former Dallas safety, in 1994*

THE RECORD

YEAR	TEAM	G	ATT	COMP	COMP%	YDS	TD	INT	RATING
1989	Dall	11	293	155	52.9	1749	9	18	55.7
1990	Dall	15	399	226	56.6	2579	11	18	66.6
1991	Dall	12	363	237	65.3	2754	11	10	86.7
1992	Dall	16	473	302	63.8	3445	23	14	89.5
1993	Dall	14	392	271	69.1	3100	15	6	99.0
1994	Dall	14	361	233	64.5	2676	13	12	84.9
1995	Dall	16	432	280	64.8	3304	16	7	93.7
1996	Dall	15	465	296	63.7	3126	12	13	80.1
1997	Dall	16	518	292	56.4	3283	19	12	78.0
1998	Dall	11	315	187	59.4	2330	12	5	88.6
TOTAL		140	4011	2479	61.8	28,346	141	115	82.8

in SI's words

Troy was 12 when his family moved to a 172-acre parcel of land near Henryetta [Okla.] to fulfull his father's dream of operating a ranch.....

Before school in the mornings Troy fed slop to the pigs. In the summer he hauled hay in the fields, often late into the night. His best class was typing, and there he had no peer. One year he won a typing contest at a place called

Okmulgee State Tech, producing 75 words a minute. He was a good player on a mediocre football team—the Henryetta Figthting Hens, they were then called. (Now they're the Knights.) Fans of opposing teams tossed rubber chickens onto the field when the Hens ran out to battle.

Nonetheless, Troy was eager for fame to find him. By the time he was a junior, folks in Oklahoma recognized

his name as belonging to the tall string bean of a kid with the amazing right arm. In 1984 Oklahoma University invited Troy to a summer football camp, and though the wishbone had long been the Sooners' offense of choice, a passing talent like Aikman's was too special for the coach—[Barry] Switzer—to ignore.

—John Ed Bradley, January 15, 1996

day practically fill the ranks of the best quarterbacks who ever gripped a football.

By way of example, let's do a little exercise here. Let's stage a draft. We'll take all the very good quarterbacks who played in the late 20th century, and then we'll ask the following question: Knowing everything that you now know about these players, in what order would you select them?

The available quarterbacks: Troy Aikman, John Elway, Brett Favre, Dan Fouts, Jim Kelly, Dan Marino, Joe Montana, Warren Moon, Phil Simms, and Steve Young.

Talk about a quarterback class. After licking my chops, I would select in the following order:

1. Montana.
2. Elway.
3. Marino.
4. Young.

Those are pretty solid. I might pick Elway ahead of Montana because with his mobility, he might stay healthy longer.

5. Favre.
6. Aikman.

For me, Aikman's lack of mobility puts him here. Favre's no track star himself, but his ability to escape beats Aikman's.

7. Fouts.
8. Kelly.
9. Simms.
10. Moon.

One negative with these lists is that they suggest you're denigrating guys you rank lower. But we're talking about la crème de la crème here, let's not forget. Aikman is among the top 1% of quarterbacks ever to play. That's saying something.

When it comes to moving the ball, Aikman has always preferred the air—the mode he chose against the Redskins in 1994 (above)—to the ground, over which he reluctantly scurried against the Niners in '96 (opposite).

marksmanship and consistency you simply can't teach.

So we return to the question I raised in the introduction to this section: If Aikman's such a winner and such a coach's quarterback and so successful, then why is he behind most of the good quarterbacks of his day? Simple. The good quarterbacks of his

Aikman

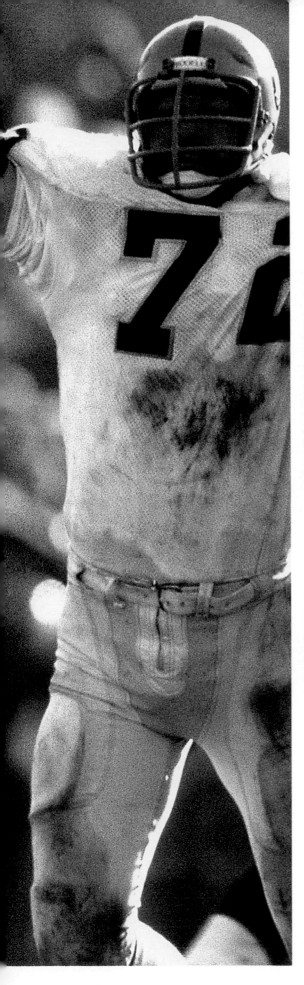

15 FranTarkenton

His teams never won a championship, but his frenetic style mesmerized spectators—and defenses

Tarkenton's exciting style of play and his ability to make mediocre teams better than they had any right to be place him (opposite, in 1977, and left, in '62) among the alltime greats.

In the mid-1990s an NFL assistant coach was talking about Steve Young, and he said, "There hasn't been a quarterback who could do as many things as well as Steve since Tarkenton."

In 1999, when the Washington Redskins were preparing to face Buffalo and its lightning-bug quarterback Doug Flutie, defensive assistant Bill Arnsparger, 73, schooled his team to play Flutie the way his Dolphin defenses played against Tarkenton in the '70s. Nonetheless, Flutie ate them alive,

both running and throwing, and the Bills won the game 34–17.

There's a lesson there, one many football aficionados have ignored—and lived to regret—over the years: Don't underestimate a player just because he's small; small players can make it in the National Football League. They can do more than make it. Case in point: Fran Tarkenton.

But before we sing his praises, let's address the anti-Tarkenton stuff first. He led the Minnesota Vikings to three Super Bowls and they lost all three.

> **"To get to play on the same team with him, work with him, catch passes from him—that's been like a dream. I hate to see him quit. There'll be a void here and in the whole NFL."**
>
> —Ahmad Rashad,
> *Vikings wide receiver, in response to Tarkenton's retirement in 1979*

Critics said he couldn't win the big one. They further charged that his scrambling style never allowed his teams, the Vikings and Giants, to build consistent offenses because everything they did on offense was crazy-quilt. They also claimed that at 6', 185 pounds (both figures were probably exaggerated), he wasn't built to take the pounding a quarterback had to take to win in the NFL.

Hey, Flutie was exiled to Canada for

THE RECORD

YEAR	TEAM	G	ATT	COMP	COMP%	YDS	TD	INT	RATING
1961	Minn	14	280	157	56.1	1997	18	17	74.7
1962	Minn	14	329	163	49.5	2595	22	25	66.9
1963	Minn	14	297	170	57.2	2311	15	15	78.0
1964	Minn	14	306	171	55.9	2506	22	11	91.8
1965	Minn	14	329	171	52.0	2609	19	11	83.8
1966	Minn	14	358	192	53.6	2561	17	16	73.8
1967	NYG	14	377	204	54.1	3088	29	19	85.9
1968	NYG	14	337	182	54.0	2555	21	12	84.6
1969	NYG	14	409	220	53.8	2918	23	8	87.2
1970	NYG	14	389	219	56.3	2777	19	12	82.2
1971	NYG	13	386	226	58.5	2567	11	21	65.4
1972	Minn	14	378	215	56.9	2651	18	13	80.2
1973	Minn	14	274	169	61.7	2113	15	7	93.2
1974	Minn	13	351	199	56.7	2598	17	12	82.1
1975	Minn	14	425	273	64.2	2994	25	13	91.8
1976	Minn	13	412	255	61.9	2961	17	8	89.3
1977	Minn	9	258	155	60.1	1734	9	14	69.2
1978	Minn	16	572	345	60.3	3468	25	32	68.9
TOTAL		246	6467	3686	57.0	47,003	342	266	80.4

Whether with the Vikings (above, in 1977) or the Giants (right, in '67), Tarkenton was a master improviser, able to conjure successful plays out of thin air.

eight years because of similar criticisms, and he's currently proving the critics wrong at age 37. In other words, bunk. Absolute bunk.

I could be biased because I grew up a New York Giants' fan in Connecticut, but I remember my family being glued to the TV on Sundays while Tarkenton gave us hope for our beloved but hapless Giants. I was 10 when the Vikings

traded him to New York. For the next five years, the Giants went 33–37. History therefore says that the Grand Tarkenton Experiment failed in New York. I say it succeeded. So does the center of those teams, Greg Larson. "In a couple of those years," Larson said, "we wouldn't have won a game without Tarkenton."

While the basic tenet of this book—that to be one of the best handful of quarterbacks in history you had to win the very big games—bars them from the very top of our rankings, men like Dan Fouts and Sonny Jurgensen and Fran Tarkenton are knocking on the door to the elite clubhouse. Because they, along with Dan Marino, are the best quarterbacks without a championship.

Tarkenton retired after playing 18 seasons, 13 with the Vikings bookending five with the Giants. He left with the league quarterbacking records for games (246) completions (3,686) attempts (6,467), yards (47,003), rushing yards (3,674) and touchdown passes (342) in his possession. As the NFL entered a pass-happy era in the 1980s and '90s, it is significant to know that every one of those records lasted at least 10 years.

The name of Tarkenton's game was improvisation. He called his own plays, initially battling with Minnesota coach Norm Van Brocklin over his tendency to leave the pocket so much. Van Brocklin believed only bad things happened when a quarterback ran out of the pocket. Tarkenton proved that magical things could happen. In the first game of his rookie year (1961) against league power Chicago, Tarkenton relieved an ineffective George Shaw at quarterback and passed for four touch-

When Tarkenton (above, versus the Packers, and opposite, versus the Raiders) was in the game, opposing defenses never knew what to expect; if they foiled the play he called, he would find another way to beat them.

downs and ran for a fifth, leading Minnesota to a 37–13 win. The game is still easily the most impressive debut by an expansion team.

Tarkenton prided himself on making great plays out of apparent disasters, and NFL Films has an incredible sequence of him as a Viking getting hemmed in, sprinting to his right, getting hemmed in again, doing a 180 and sprinting back to his left, where he was once again trapped, then winding up and uncorking a long completion to wide receiver Ahmad Rashad. The play must have lasted 25 seconds, and that's why a Tarkenton game was

supportingcast

While Fran Tarkenton was certainly a magician, he had no shortage of assistants to help him pull off his sleight of hand. And of all his weapons, none served Tarkenton better than his longtime backfield mate Chuck Foreman.

Foreman was the Vikings No. 1 draft pick in 1973 and he immediately made his mark as one of the most versatile running backs in the league. His spinning, churning running style produced three consecutive 1,000-yard seasons (1975–77), but it was his pass catching skills that made him such a headache for defenses and a godsend for Tarkenton. In 1975, Foreman had an NFL-leading 73 receptions, nine of which went for touchdowns. He also rushed for 13 scores. Rather than constantly scrambling for his life, waiting for someone to get open and risking a sack as in the past, Tarkenton could now dump off a short pass to Foreman. Head Coach Bud Grant described Foreman's talents thusly, "We know that Chuck can get five yards on a running play so we throw him a five-yard pass and let him get even more. It is just an extension of our running game."

In the six years he played with Tarkenton, Foreman had 317 receptions for 23 touchdowns.

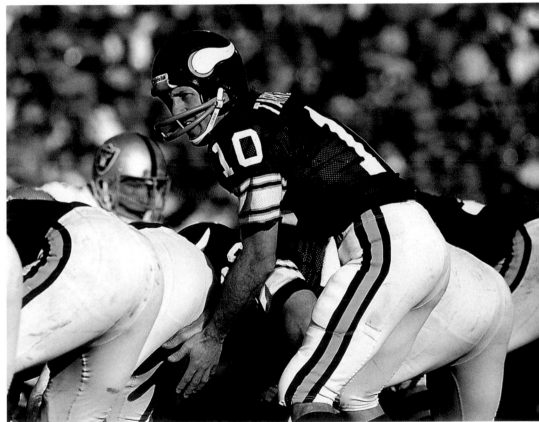

so exciting, regardless of the outcome.

In his last year, when he was 38, Tarkenton called an option play in a game against Detroit. Before Tarkenton was able to pitch the ball, Detroit defensive tackle Dave Pureifory steamed in and blasted him, helmet-to-chin. Tarkenton's head snapped back violently, and three of his front teeth popped out and landed on the ground.

Tarkenton saw stars. He hopped to his feet, put his arm on Pureifory's shoulder and lisped: "No hard feelings, Dave. I'm okay already." He played the second half. The Vikings won 17–7. After the game, Tarkenton had three hours of plastic surgery and took 60 stitches. Then two hours of dental work.

"He's the greatest quarterback ever to play the game," said his longtime coach, Bud Grant.

I won't go that far, but he's in the same class as the greats.

16 SonnyJurgensen

A rowdy character in the mold of Bobby Layne, Jurgensen joins Dan Marino as the best quarterbacks who never won a title

Sadly, the last game of Sonny Jurgensen's 18-year NFL career was his first playoff game. Jurgensen had an arm like a crossbow. He once quarterbacked the Redskins to a 72–41 win over the Giants. He played for the Eagles when they won the NFL title in 1960, but he was the backup behind Norm Van Brocklin. When he joined the Redskins they were in the midst of their horrid years, and he just couldn't lift bad teams out of their doldrums, no matter how hard he threw, or how many times.

If Jurgensen found your weakness, God help you. It was much the same with Otto Graham, Jurgy's coach in Washington for three years. "The only difference between Otto and me," said Jurgensen, "is he likes candy bars and milkshakes, and I like women and scotch." The NFL fined him $500 for that one. Jurgensen, it was reported, laughed when he heard the news of the fine.

It was a different era. A good number of quarterbacks today don't drink anything but protein shakes during the week. I once followed the supposedly wild Brett Favre for a week in 1995, even joined him on a hunting trip on his day off, and only saw him drink once—after the game on Sunday, in his basement.

Sonny was a different story. He let a

The fun-loving Jurgensen (above, in 1974 and opposite, in 1969) was among the finest pure passers in NFL history; only a weak supporting cast kept him from accomplishing more.

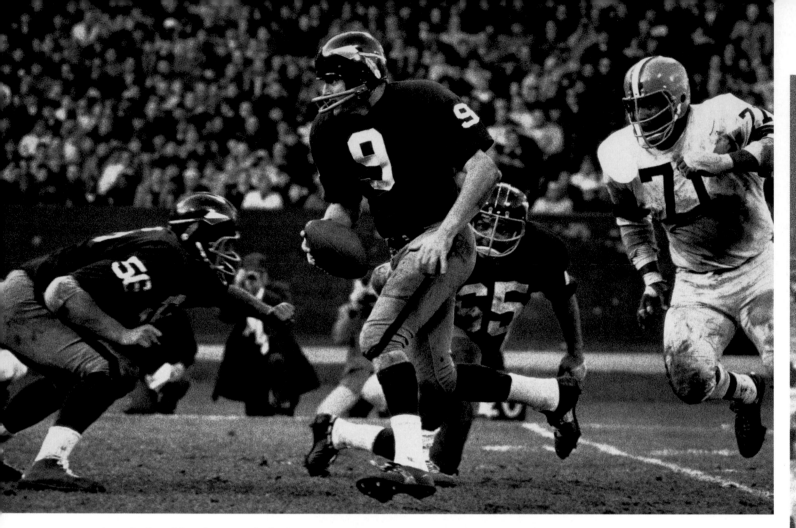

Slow of foot and weighed down even further by bulky protective vests, Jurgensen out of the pocket (above, in 1967) was easy prey for the likes of Washington tackle Joe Rutgens (opposite, right).

writer shadow him for a week during the 1968 season, and subscribers read about Monday afternoon Bloody Marys, followed by Cutty Sark and water in the evening and more Cutty and water at home at night. How many did he have? Plenty. On Thursday evening, he was back at his favorite watering hole. He was a carouser, and he kept it up for some time. "When I left Philadelphia," he said, "the bartenders all wore black armbands."

Who knows how good Jurgensen would have been if he'd been a teetotaler, or on a great team, or even a pretty good one?

After the 1969 season, in which Jurgensen completed 62% of his passes and threw for 22 touchdowns, new Washington coach Vince Lombardi told him, "If we'd had you in Green Bay, we never would have lost." But the Skins had gone

THE RECORD

YEAR	TEAM	G	ATT	COMP	COMP%	YDS	TD	INT	RATING
1957	Phil	10	70	33	47.1	470	5	8	53.6
1958	Phil	12	22	12	54.5	259	0	1	77.7
1959	Phil	12	5	3	60.0	27	1	0	114.2
1960	Phil	12	44	24	54.5	486	5	1	122.0
1961	Phil	14	416	235	56.5	3723	32	24	88.1
1962	Phil	14	366	196	53.6	3261	22	26	74.3
1963	Phil	9	184	99	53.8	1413	11	13	69.4
1964	Wash	14	385	207	53.8	2934	24	13	85.4
1965	Wash	13	356	190	53.4	2367	15	16	69.6
1966	Wash	14	436	254	58.3	3209	28	19	84.5
1967	Wash	14	508	288	56.7	3747	31	16	87.3
1968	Wash	12	292	167	57.2	1980	17	11	81.7
1969	Wash	14	442	272	62.0	3102	22	15	85.4
1970	Wash	14	337	202	59.9	2354	23	10	91.5
1971	Wash	5	28	16	57.1	170	0	2	45.2
1972	Wash	7	59	39	66.1	633	2	4	84.9
1973	Wash	14	145	87	60.0	904	6	5	77.5
1974	Wash	14	167	107	64.1	1185	11	5	94.5
TOTAL		218	4262	2433	57.1	32,224	255	189	82.6

7-5-2 that year and missed the playoffs.

Jurgensen's brilliance was hard to hide, though, even if the players around him couldn't come close to matching it. The images of Jurgensen from his Washington days, (1964 to '74), show a

slow—glacially slow—man with 18 extra pounds spread across his midsection, looking like a barkeep from Bethesda instead of a quarterback for the beloved Skins. The film shows a man who could throw a football two

Jurgensen

A Jurgensen spiral such as the one above was a thing of beauty; unfortunately, Jurgensen (opposite, in 1968) was often sacked before he could hurl one of his majestic rainbows skyward.

ways: like a frozen rope, or in a high, arcing rainbow. With a perfect spiral either way. In 1961, his first season as a starter, he set an NFL record with 3,723 passing yards. He improved from there. But if he didn't score 28 by himself, the Redskins usually lost.

I went back over Jurgensen's career, looking at his numbers in the days when the Redskins were truly awful. I looked at 1967 and caught a glimpse of Washington's maddening inconsistency. One week, the Redskins tied the Fal-

cons 20–20. The Falcons were in their second year of existence and would finish the season 1-12-1. The next week Washington tied the Rams 28–28. Los Angeles would tie the Colts for the league's best record, 11-1-2. Jurgensen threw four touchdown passes and no interceptions against the Rams that day.

Late in that season Jurgensen threw 50 passes in a game two weeks in a row. He completed 32 of them the first week against Cleveland, for 418 yards

> "Never, ever have I seen anyone throw a prettier ball. I still think he may have been the best pure passer in history."
>
> —Joe Theismann, *former Redskins quarterback, in 1991*

supportingcast

While it is well documented that Sonny Jurgensen did not play for the finest teams, he nonetheless needed some talented offensive players—some talented receivers in particular—to help him rack up 32,224 career passing yards. One such crucial supporter was Hall of Fame wide receiver Charley Taylor.

Taylor joined the Redskins as a first-round draft pick in 1964, which was also Jurgensen's first year with the club. Though he was used primarily as a running back in his first two seasons, it soon became apparent that Taylor's real talent was as a receiver. In the seventh game of 1966 he was made a full-time split end and flourished in the role, leading the league in catches in both 1966 (72) and '67 (70). Such impressive numbers notwithstanding, the Redskins failed to make the playoffs in either season.

Taylor retired in 1977 as the NFL's all-time leading receiver, with 649 catches for 9,110 yards and 79 touchdowns, most of them the result of Jurgensen tosses. Even though they couldn't lift the Redskins to a championship, both men certainly spurred each other to greatness.

and three touchdowns, and Washington lost 42–37. He completed 30 of them the following week, for 366 yards and four touchdowns. That got the Skins a 35–35 tie with the Eagles, who were just as bad as Washington was. "It's pretty tough when you know you've probably got to score 40 every week to have a good chance to win," Jurgensen said. "Also, because we got behind so much and teams knew we were going to pass a lot, I got beat up. There were times I played with a fiberglass vest. It was like wearing a suit of armor. If I ever tried to run, the defense laughed."

Players like Jurgensen remind me not to be so absolute in my judgment of quarterbacks on winning alone. It takes a well-rounded team to succeed in the NFL; one guy, no matter how good he is, can't do it alone. Jurgensen may bear some of the blame for his teams' poor showings, but my (rather large) gut tells me that this hard drinker with the outsized belly—and talent to match—ranks with the greatest quarterbacks of all time.

17 DanFouts

He succeeded a legend and became one.
No Super Bowls. Just a super player.

Despite having the prolific Fouts at quarterback, the Chargers were rarely able to transcend mediocrity, going 8–8 in 1985 (opposite) and 8–7 in the strike-shortened '87 season (right), after which Fouts called an end to his 15-year career.

Dan Fouts was a steely, no-excuses, golden-armed quarterback who got about the best training in quarterbacking a kid could ever get. His dad, Bob Fouts, worked as the 49ers' play-by-play man while Dan was growing up in San Francisco, and so Dan landed a job as ballboy. He saw the good and bad—mostly bad, because the 49ers were lousy back then—of life as an NFL quarterback as lived by San Francisco QB John Brodie. And Fouts became like Brodie: Good leader, deaf to boos, very smart player, and tough. The only difference was Fouts's arm. Brodie's was NFL-quality, to be sure, but Fouts's was like a laser-guided cannon.

In 1973 the Chargers picked Fouts out of Oregon in the third round. At halftime of the fifth game of his rookie year, the aging Johnny Unitas was pulled from the San Diego lineup for good with the Chargers trailing Pittsburgh 38–0. Fouts came in and spearheaded three scoring drives. San Diego lost 38–21, but Fouts had won the job, long before anyone thought he would.

And like Sonny Jurgensen from the previous generation, Fouts would spend year after frustrating year trying to score enough points to cover for the swiss-cheese defense the Chargers fielded every season. Just look at the Chargers-Raiders series during Fouts's prime. Here's a sampling of final scores from the 14 games they played between 1979 and 1985: 45–22, 38–24, 55–21, 41–34, 33–30, 44–37, 40–34. And so on. Seven of the 14 games during that span produced more than 60 points. Nowadays, maybe one NFL game every three weeks will yield 60 points. "I start preparing for the two San Diego games in June," said the Raiders' star cornerback from that era, Lester Hayes. "I look at Dan Fouts films going back to 1976. The more I watch them, the more I see that the fear factor simply is not there. The man does not fear any defensive back."

Fouts used to hold the ball until the last second before getting hit because that's what a quarterback was supposed to do: Fear no one, be immune to pain, take

"Dan is just a natural leader. In the huddle he's in charge. The guys like him and respect him and I think he feels the same about them."

—Joe Gibbs, *former Chargers offensive coordinator, in 1979*

Fouts

THE RECORD

YEAR	TEAM	G	ATT	COMP	COMP%	YDS	TD	INT	RATING
1973	SD	10	194	87	44.8	1126	6	13	46.0
1974	SD	11	237	115	48.5	1732	8	13	61.4
1975	SD	10	195	106	54.4	1396	2	10	59.3
1976	SD	14	359	208	57.9	2535	14	15	75.4
1977	SD	4	109	69	63.3	869	4	6	77.4
1978	SD	15	381	224	58.8	2999	24	20	83.0
1979	SD	16	530	332	62.6	4082	24	24	82.6
1980	SD	16	589	348	59.1	4715	30	24	84.7
1981	SD	16	609	360	59.1	4802	33	17	90.6
1982	SD	9	330	204	61.8	2883	17	11	93.3
1983	SD	10	340	215	63.2	2975	20	15	92.5
1984	SD	13	507	317	62.5	3740	19	17	83.4
1985	SD	14	430	254	59.1	3638	27	20	88.1
1986	SD	12	430	252	58.6	3031	16	22	71.4
1987	SD	11	364	206	56.6	2517	10	15	70.0
TOTAL		181	5604	3297	58.8	43,040	254	242	80.2

Dangerous Dan: Fouts had arguably his best year ever in 1981 (above), when he passed for 4,802 yards and 33 touchdowns and led the Chargers to the AFC title game; but only two years later (opposite), San Diego was back in the doldrums, going 6–10.

it like a man, and even dish it out when necessary. "He was a workhorse," said future Hall of Fame safety Ronnie Lott. "Dan would have been a great defensive lineman. There was nothing out there that got him, nothing he couldn't handle."

Fouts's tremendous aggression was always channeled, never out of control. Bill Walsh spent one year, 1976, as the Chargers offensive coordinator, and he knew when he walked into the organization that there was loads of pressure on Fouts. The Chargers had gone 2–12 the previous season. Fouts had a nearly identical line that year: two touchdowns, 10 interceptions. So when Walsh came to work in the offseason, Fouts did too, with newspaper gossip that the Chargers were looking to trade him swirling around him.

Fouts was not particularly agile but he wasn't afraid to stand tall in the pocket until the last possible instant to unleash his catapault of an arm, as he demonstrated in 1984 against Houston (left) and in '81 versus the Chiefs (above).

Fouts

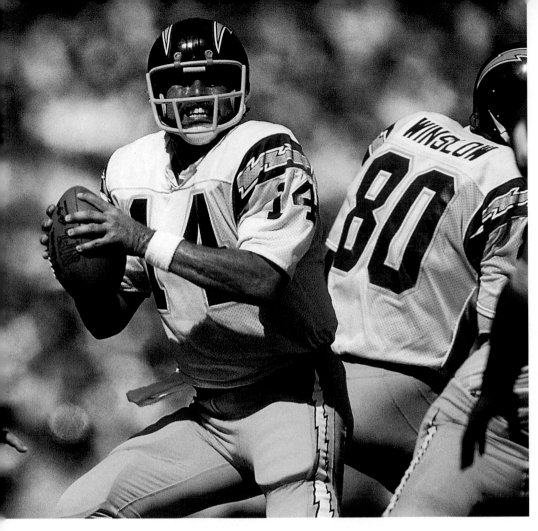

He turned his game over to Walsh. He adjusted his footwork. He adjusted his mechanics. He worked to improve the timing on his passes, so as not to zig when his receivers zagged. He studied the game like never before. When Don Coryell began his first full season as coach in 1979, Fouts was a mature passer in the Walsh mold. He threw 24, 30, 33 and 17 touchdown passes over the next four years, with that last total coming in a strike-shortened season. In the 1981 playoffs, in the heat of the Orange Bowl, he quarterbacked the Chargers to one of the biggest wins in franchise history, a game that ranks with the most exciting of all time. He passed for 433 yards and three touchdowns, and the Chargers won a see-saw affair over the Dolphins, 41–38 in overtime.

In 1982, when they were on the verge of greatness (they would never get there), the Chargers went to San Francisco to face the defending champs. This was the year of the NFL strike, with the schedule cut to nine games, but this matchup would be the belle of the ball: the can't-miss contest of the year—Fouts versus Joe Montana, the wünderkind.

Fouts strafed the great San Francisco secondary. He found wideout Wes Chandler deep and tight end Kellen Winslow over the middle and running back Chuck Muncie in the flat and receiver Charlie Joiner everywhere. Fouts connected on 33 of 48 passes for 450 yards and five touchdowns. San Diego won a shootout 41–37.

"When you went up against the Chargers and Fouts," cornerback Eric Wright said, "you knew it was going to be bombs away."

And that's how you should remember Dan Fouts.

supportingcast

Perhaps no other game better illustrates the high-flying air show of Dan Fouts and the San Diego Chargers of the '80s—and the sterling support Fouts received from his all-world tight end Kellen Winslow—than their thrilling 41–38 overtime win over the Miami Dolphins in the AFC divisional playoffs on January 2, 1982.

Only 13:29 into the game, before the Dolphins knew what had hit them, the Chargers took a 24–0 lead on the strength of a Wes Chandler punt return for a touchdown, a one-yard run by Chuck Muncie and an 8-yard pass from Fouts to James Brooks. But as Fouts and his offense were well aware, no lead was safe with the seemingly nonexistent Chargers defense.

Don Strock replaced an ineffective David Woodley at quarterback for Miami and by halftime the score was 24–17. In the second half Fouts used his full arsenal of offensive weapons, but none more than Winslow, who caught a playoff-record 13 balls for 166 yards. As players on both teams fell victim to cramps and dehydration, Fouts and Strock kept firing. Fouts would end the game with a then playoff-record 433 yards passing and three TDs and as time wound down the teams were deadlocked at 38.

At the end of regulation, Winslow blocked a potential game-winning field goal by Uwe von Schamann and the Chargers went on to win in overtime on Rolf Benirschke's 29-yard boot. At first glance, the final score would appear to be yet another typical Chargers game. But Coryell rightly described it as "probably the most exciting game in the history of pro football."

18 BobbyLayne

He led the Lions to all the glory the franchise has known—and had a pretty good time doing it

One night in the 1950s, Lions quarterback Bobby Layne and teammates Joe Schmidt and Gene Gedman drove to a bar in downtown Detroit. Layne couldn't find a parking spot, so he parked on the sidewalk. In most towns, that's not legal. When the police came to ticket and tow the car, Layne went out to talk to them. The next thing Schmidt and Gedman knew, Layne was getting into his car, waving for his friends to join him. They piled in, and the cops activated their lights and siren.

Layne did not receive a ticket, nor was his car towed. He did, however, get a police escort to the next bar.

"He was a one-man team who went against all the rules," Lions coach Buddy Parker said. "But by golly, it worked."

The rules said that a quarterback should be chiseled and fit; Layne was pudgy, and round enough in the middle to be taken for the guy who pumps your gas, not the one who leads your football team on Sunday afternoons. The rules said that a quarterback should be a student of the game, study films, know defenses; Layne once said, "I'm a born night owl. I start having fun at midnight, get to bed when everyone else is waking and sleep all morning." The rules said that a quarterback should project a proper image to the press; Layne once told the fourth estate, "One of the hazards of participating in sports is that you are always thrown into the company of the nation's sportswriters, a bunch of guys who can be divided into two categories: those who are looking for a headline, and those who are looking for a drink."

Traded from New York to Detroit

before the 1950 season, the 6' 1", 205-pound Layne was handed the starter's job and the task of reviving the sagging Lions, who'd lost their growl after four straight losing seasons. Layne quickly magnetized his teammates. In one of his early training camps, he showed up with a satchel containing $14,000 he had won in a Dallas poker game. "No matter what I say," he told teammate Doak Walker, handing him the bag, "only give me $500 a day."

Soon afterward, Layne called Walker late one night and begged for more cash. Walker refused, saying he'd already given him $500. "But it's after midnight! It's tomorrow!" Layne squawked. Tales like that, plus Layne's selflessness and hatred of losing, endeared him to tough teammates and fans in a tough town.

If he was chased from the pocket by a defense, Layne, despite the extra baggage he carried in his midsection, liked to run, and he had one of the best arms in the league. Slightly erratic off the field, he was surprisingly accurate on it; his spirals feathered down into the hands of his receivers, and he was at his best when his back was against the wall.

It took only three years of the Layne Era for the Lions to win an NFL title. They defeated league powerhouse Cleveland 17–7 in the 1952 title game as Layne ran for Detroit's first score. The next season brought the same championship matchup, and the Browns led the Lions 16–10 with four minutes to play. Layne took over on the Detroit 20-yard line. "Y'all block," the Texan drawled to his offensive linemen, "and ol' Bobby'll pass you to a championship."

Less than two minutes later, he made good on his promise, finishing the

Sometimes even Layne had to hand off (above); in 1954, Layne (opposite, against the Rams) threw for 1818 yards but the Lions lost to the mighty Browns in the NFL title game.

THE RECORD

YEAR	TEAM	G	ATT	COMP	COMP%	YDS	TD	INT	RATING
1948	ChiB	11	52	16	30.8	232	3	2	49.5
1949	NYB	12	299	155	51.8	1796	9	18	55.3
1950	Det	12	336	152	45.2	2323	16	18	62.1
1951	Det	12	332	152	45.8	2403	26	23	67.6
1952	Det	12	287	139	48.4	1999	19	20	64.5
1953	Det	12	273	125	45.8	2088	16	21	59.6
1954	Det	12	246	135	54.9	1818	14	12	77.3
1955	Det	12	270	143	53.0	1830	11	17	61.8
1956	Det	12	244	129	52.9	1909	9	17	62.0
1957	Det	11	179	87	48.6	1169	6	12	53.0
1958	Det/Pitt	12	294	145	49.3	2510	14	12	77.6
1959	Pitt	12	297	142	47.8	1986	20	21	62.8
1960	Pitt	12	209	103	49.3	1814	13	17	66.2
1961	Pitt	8	149	75	50.3	1205	11	16	62.8
1962	Pitt	13	233	116	49.8	1686	9	17	56.2
TOTAL		175	3700	1814	49.0	26,768	196	243	63.4

80-yard drive with a 33-yard scoring strike to wideout Jim Doran. That was the second of three titles Layne delivered to Detroit, and the hardscrabble city warmly adopted him. "He was the symbol of the city, the toughest and the best," *Detroit News* columnist Jerry Green once wrote. "When a touchdown drive was necessary, he could make two minutes seem an eternity."

The late sportswriter Jim Murray summed up Layne even more poignantly on the occasion of the Hall of Famer's death in 1986: "He never called timeout unless somebody's ear

aftermath

Bobby Layne followed former Lions coach Buddy Parker to the Pittsburgh Steelers in 1958 with hopes of bestowing a championship upon that team—reasonable enough given Layne's heroic achievements in Detroit. But Pittsburgh had enjoyed only three winning records in its 24-year history. And while Layne immediately created the same kind of on- and off-the-field excitement that had made him an icon in Detroit and helped the Steelers to three above-.500 seasons in the five years before he retired in 1962, he came up short on his championship promise.

After years of milking every second from the clock, the consummate partier was unable to rally when liver disease and other health problems caught up with him in 1986. He died at age 59. As Lions teammate Doak Walker said, "Bobby never lost a game in his life. Time just ran out on him." In Layne's 15 years of pro football, he connected on 1,814 of 3,700 passes for 26,768 yards and 196 touchdowns. He also kicked 34 field goals and made good on 120 extra points for a total of 372 points. An All-Pro in 1952 and 1956, Layne became a Hall-of-Famer in 1967.

"He's a case of don't-do-as-I-do, but do-as-I-tell-you. He's a one-man team who goes against all the rules. But by golly, it works."

—Buddy Parker,
former Lions coach, in 1960

Layne

was bleeding or lung was showing, never just to get a play from the bench. He could score quickly if he had to, but his specialty was using precisely as much time as he had on the clock to win and prevent the other team from retaliating.... Bobby went through his whole life on audibles. He didn't think real men went to bed before the bars closed or the chips ran out. His football teams would have gone through a forest fire for him. He used to bark signals in that laryngitic rasp that sounded as if someone had him by the throat or his collar was too tight. He was a leader.... In his eight years with the Lions, they won three championship and four division titles. There were only two divisions in those days. They have won none since."

Detroit won division titles in 1991 and 1993, but didn't go all the way in either year. They haven't had a great quarterback since; they'll never have another one like Layne.

Layne and the Lions entered the 1954 title game (above) against the Browns riding a four-game winning streak against Otto Graham's talented team, but it was the Browns who cruised to an easy victory, 56–10; by 1959, Layne (opposite) had been traded to Pittsburgh.

19 JimKelly

While leading Buffalo to four consecutive AFC titles, he may have been the most innovative quarterback of his day

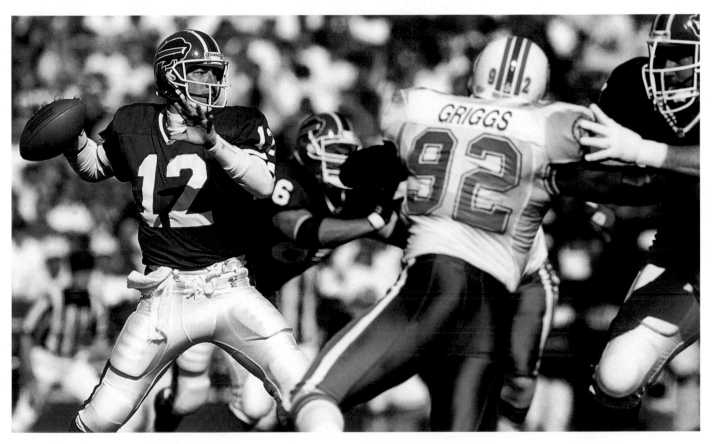

To understand what Jim Kelly did in Buffalo—with a little help from Marv Levy, Bruce Smith and friends—you first have to understand the fishbowl–style pressure, from fans, the media and the competition, of pro football from 1980 to 2000.

The Buffalo Bills drafted the University of Miami star in 1983, but he chose the absurd money offered to him by the Houston Gamblers of the new United States Football League instead of the merely astronomical money he could have earned with Buffalo, which was lost and wander-

ing in the NFL wilderness at the time.

So Kelly joined Houston of the soon-to-be-defunct USFL, and threw 83 touchdown passes in two years. Meanwhile, the Bills had 2–14 records in stereo.

In August 1986, after the USFL's weak antitrust case against the NFL led to its demise, the Bills reached an agreement on a contract with Kelly. When he drove in from the airport to sign the deal, fans hung signs on overpasses welcoming Kelly to town. The governor of New York, Mario Cuomo, flew from Albany to welcome Kelly at a luncheon. Before his first game, against the Jets, a

The Bills under Kelly (opposite, versus the Jets in 1986, and above, versus Miami in 1992) were a regular-season juggernaut, going 49–15 over one four-season stretch; it was only in the Super Bowl that the team lost steam.

fan hung a sign in Rich Stadium that read: JIM KELLY IS GOD.

Pressure? Nah, all Kelly had to do was go out and win two or three championships and the fans would be happy. No problem.

Kelly won four championships. AFC championships, that is. But he was 0 for 4 in the Super Bowl, and he played poorly in two of those games, just so-so in the other two. That has led some to say, Kelly put up good numbers, but a guy who gets to the Super Bowl four times and doesn't win once? Can't be one of the greats.

A little perspective, please.

The single damnable transgression in Kelly's career was that he was lousy in Super Bowls. The Bills lost the four Big Ones by an embarrassing average of 16.5 points per game, and most of Kelly's moments of success came after the games had already been decided. Outside of garbage time, he threw zero touchdowns and was intercepted seven times in the

THE RECORD

YEAR	TEAM	G	ATT	COMP	COMP%	YDS	TD	INT	RATING
1986	Buff	16	480	285	59.4	3593	22	17	83.3
1987	Buff	12	419	250	59.7	2798	19	11	83.8
1988	Buff	16	452	269	59.5	3380	15	17	78.2
1989	Buff	13	391	228	58.3	3130	25	18	86.2
1990	Buff	14	346	219	63.3	2829	24	9	101.2
1991	Buff	15	474	304	64.1	3844	33	17	97.6
1992	Buff	16	462	269	58.2	3457	23	19	81.2
1993	Buff	16	470	288	61.3	3382	18	18	79.9
1994	Buff	14	448	285	63.6	3114	22	17	84.6
1995	Buff	15	458	255	55.7	3130	22	13	81.1
1996	Buff	13	379	222	58.6	2810	14	19	73.2
TOTAL		160	4779	2874	60.1	35,467	237	175	84.4

Big, strong and mobile, Kelly (above, in 1991, and opposite, versus the Cowboys in Super Bowl XXVII) could take an NFL licking and keep on ticking as well as any quarterback in history.

Kelly

four losses. You can't erase those failures when you consider the career of Kelly.

But if he hadn't bombed in Super Bowls, he'd be higher on this list, probably in the Top 10. Consider what he did well. More than any player in Buffalo, he took the worst franchise—by far—in the AFC and made it one of the best teams the conference had seen in the last 20 years of the century. A 6' 3" ruffian who could—and had to, considering Buffalo's porous pass-protection in his early days—take a pounding as well as any quarterback of his day, Kelly missed only 14 starts in 11 years because of injuries.

No wonder, coming from a guy that some college coaches—Joe Paterno of Penn State among them—recruited as a linebacker. In Buffalo, he became the rugged engineer of a unique offense, driving the Bills to eight playoff appearances in nine years. In his four Super Bowl seasons, Kelly led his team on an Otto Graham–esque, 49–15 tear in the regular season.

The no-huddle was his métier. Kelly had free rein to audible and call his own plays. The Bills, in these glory years, went whole series at a time without huddling, and Kelly ran the show. He used hand signals to wave in different player groupings, and hand or verbal signals to call plays and position

in SI's words

A crowd of 18,828 allegedly saw Jim Kelly beat the Los Angeles Express 34–33 at the L.A. Coliseum on Feb. 24, 1985. The USFL belongs to the school of creative attendance counting, wherein seat backs often become human beings—but whoever or whatever watched Kelly in the fourth quarter that day got a treat. With the [Houston-New Jersey] Gamblers down 33–13 and about nine minutes left in the game, Kelly threw touchdown passes of 52, 40 and 39 yards in a total of 12 offensive plays consuming 208 seconds. The empty stadium echoed with silence. But it was a performance that transcended the boundaries of a lousy league. Even if the Express had tombstones for defensive backs, it was some display. "I didn't even think we'd get the ball three times," says Gamblers-Generals offensive coordinator John Jenkins. For the game Kelly completed 35 of 54 passes for 574 yards and 5 TDs. It was a good day for him, but not unexpected.

In 1984, his first season in the USFL, Kelly threw for 5,219 yards and 44 touchdowns, more in each category than any rookie in any league. Until Dan Marino threw 48 TD passes later that year, no one at all had connected on more scoring strikes in a season than Kelly....
—Rick Telander, July 21, 1986

A master of the audible, Kelly (above and left, versus San Francisco in 1992) made the defense-befuddling no-huddle offense a major new weapon in the pro football arsenal.

players in the right spots. All of this, of course, was to unsettle the defense. The opposition couldn't substitute without the time a huddle provides to shuffle players in and out, and even if they found the time they couldn't be sure which players to bring in because they couldn't guess what was coming amidst the confusing movement and signaling on the other side of the ball.

In 1990, Kelly served notice that he was running the most dominant offense in the league. Buffalo's playoff opponents that January were Miami and the Raiders, both of whom ranked near the top in the NFL in team defense and scor-

ing defense. The Bills scored 44 points against the Dolphins, and, in an incredible display of offensive firepower, shot out to a 41–3 lead in the first half against the Raiders before going on to win 51–3.

"What I love about this offense," Kelly said, "is I can figure out from being on the field what's working and what isn't, and then I can go exploit it. But none of it would be possible if I didn't have the talent around me to make it work."

That talent, though, didn't throw for more yards than Sonny Jurgensen or more touchdowns than Terry Bradshaw. Kelly did, which is why he has a well-deserved spot among our Top 20.

20 PhilSimms

A quarterbacking chameleon who put the team first with his willingness to do whatever it took to win

Just Win, Baby: Simms (opposite, in Super Bowl XXI, and left in 1984) was one quarterback on our list who was willing to do anything to win, even if it meant taking a back seat in a ball-control offense.

While he was coaching the New York Giants Bill Parcells once borrowed a sportswriter's team media guide and opened it up to the year-by-year results section. "You know, when people look back at how a team did," Parcells said, pointing to the rows and rows of wins and losses, "they don't want to know, 'Who was hurt that day?' Or: 'Did you have all your horses?' They don't care how you won. They just want to know: 'Did you win the game or not?'"

Parcells has always espoused this as the beauty of football. No excuses. No explanations. "And that," he continued that day, "is the reason why I'm glad Simms is my quarterback. He doesn't care how he gets it done. He just cares that it gets done."

Simms may be the most surprising choice for this Top 20, and I must admit I might not have him here if I hadn't covered him for four years of his prime while I was working for *Newsday*. He helped the Giants to Super Bowl wins after the 1986 and '90 seasons, though a broken foot prevented him from playing the last five games of 1990. When he retired in 1994 he was 11th alltime in passing yardage, despite playing for a ball-control team his entire career.

But stats don't tell the whole story with Simms. As Parcells said, he did whatever would help his team win. When the Giants asked him to be a mad bomber in 1984, he was happy to oblige, passing for 4,044 yards. When they asked him to be a cog in the machine, he tucked in his ego like he

THE RECORD

YEAR	TEAM	G	ATT	COMP	COMP%	YDS	TD	INT	RATING
1979	NYG	12	265	134	50.6	1743	13	14	66.0
1980	NYG	13	402	193	48.0	2321	15	19	58.9
1981	NYG	10	316	172	54.4	2031	11	9	74.0
1982	DNP								
1983	NYG	2	13	7	53.8	130	0	1	56.6
1984	NYG	16	533	286	53.7	4044	22	18	78.1
1985	NYG	16	495	275	55.6	3829	22	20	78.6
1986	NYG	16	468	259	55.3	3487	21	22	74.6
1987	NYG	9	282	163	57.8	2230	17	9	90.0
1988	NYG	15	479	263	54.9	3359	21	11	82.1
1989	NYG	15	405	228	56.3	3061	14	14	77.6
1990	NYG	14	311	184	59.2	2284	15	4	92.7
1991	NYG	6	141	82	58.2	993	8	4	87.0
1992	NYG	4	137	83	60.6	912	5	3	83.3
1993	NYG	16	400	247	61.8	3038	15	9	88.3
TOTAL		**164**	**4647**	**2576**	**55.4**	**33,462**	**199**	**157**	**78.5**

was running a bootleg. His passing took a back seat to the running game and the Giants rose to prominence in 1985 and 1986. When they asked him to come up big in big games, he came up huge: His 22-of-25 performance (with two drops by receivers) in the Giants' 39–20 Super Bowl XXI win over Denver may never be matched. When the Giants looked at the tape of the game, they were amazed to find that 21 of Simms's 25 passes were bull's-eyes—the receivers didn't have to leap or lunge, only open their hands and welcome the ball in.

Simms also led by example. Seven days after the quarterback's brilliant Super Bowl performance, Giants strength and conditioning coach Johnny Parker walked into his house from Sunday church services to a ringing phone. He picked it up to hear Simms say: "C'mon, Johnny, let's go! A week off's enough! Let's start the offseason workouts!" A running back who asked me to keep this off the record (I'll use it now but without mentioning the name) once told me, almost embarrassed: "I would walk through fire for Simms."

Historically, maybe this Simms story works best. In 1979 Bill Walsh was looking for a quarterback to run his West Coast offense in San Francisco. He knew Washington State quarterback Jack Thompson would go high. He wasn't much of a fan of Clemson's Steve Fuller. He personally scouted and liked Simms, from Morehead State, but didn't know if he'd last until the 49ers' first turn, the 29th selection overall. He didn't. Simms went to the Giants in the first round. Walsh picked Joe Montana from Notre Dame in the third. I once asked Walsh after he'd retired from coaching

Simms (opposite, versus the Rams in 1989) was simply brilliant in Super Bowl XXI (above), completing 22 of 25 passes, a completion-percentage record in the title game that may stand for a very long time.

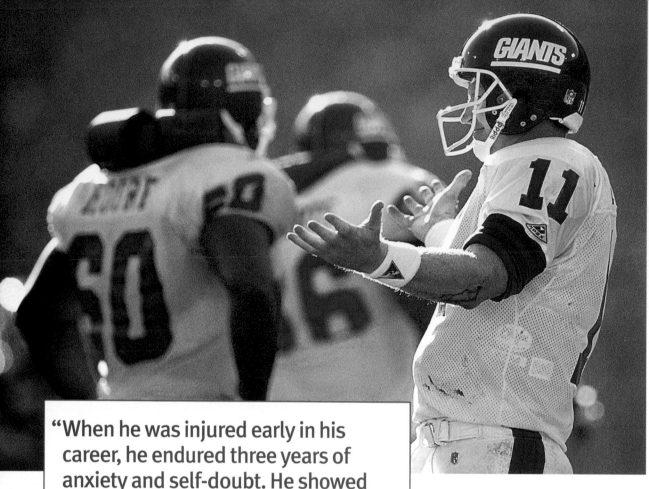

> "When he was injured early in his career, he endured three years of anxiety and self-doubt. He showed us what Phil Simms was all about. If it took the fans until now to understand, well, the taste of the American public has long been suspect."
>
> —George Young,
> *former New York Giants general manager, in 1986*

how Simms would have done in that offense. "There's no doubt in my mind, with his toughness, smarts and touch, that he would have been a great quarterback for us," Walsh said. "He might have been as good as Joe."

Simms, of course, was like any good player in any sport. He wanted the ball with the game on the line. He wanted to decide the game himself. He also realized, most times, that his coaches knew what they were doing. Letting a strong defense, great special teams and a solid running game rule the day were often the best ways for the Giants to win. "There were two things I really liked doing," Simms said after his retirement. "Playing and winning."

Two nights before Super Bowl XXI, Simms dined with the comedian Billy Crystal, a huge Giants' fan. Crystal wondered if Simms might tell him what the first play of the game would be. "Incut to Lionel Manuel," Simms said. "About 17, 20 yards. Bet on it." First play of the game at the Rose Bowl two days later: Simms drops back, Manuel runs up the right seam and breaks in at exactly 17 yards. The ball hits him in the numbers. A 17-yard incut.

At a banquet in Kansas City that winter, former Chiefs quarterback Len Dawson ran into Simms and congratulated him heartily. "Fella," Dawson told him, "I don't think they'll ever match those numbers you put up that day."

"Good," said Simms. "I hope they don't. I hope that's how I'll be remembered."

Simms' celebration in Super Bowl XXI (above) was a high point in his career; one of the lows came against San Francisco (above, left) in 1994, when the Giants lost 44–3 in the divisional playoffs.

aftermath

Phil Simms's playing career came to a surprisingly abrupt end in 1994. He had ranked fourth in the NFL in passing in 1993 and helped the Giants to an 11–5 record. But as Simms rehabilitated an injury and readied himself for the '94 season, the Giants released him. New York was hoping to get younger, and in their opinion, Simms's age, health and salary made him a risk under the new salary-cap system. After 15 years and two Super Bowl seasons, Simms found himself out of football.

He could have signed with a number of teams in the offseason, but Simms decided to retire. He studied with a media coach and joined ESPN's football coverage as a studio analyst. In 1995, he teamed with NBC's top broadcast duo of Dick Enberg and Paul McGuire and quickly established himself as one of television's most astute analysts. When CBS outbid NBC for the right to broadcast AFC football, Simms joined CBS's Greg Gumbel in the booth.

Announcing games isn't the only way that Simms has remained close to the game. His son Chris starred at Ramapo High School in New Jersey and was the most sought after high-school quarterback in the nation in 1999. The 6'5", 215-pound left-hander chose the University of Texas after a long recruiting process. Although Chris had yet to start a college game at press time, many people thought he had the size, ability, and bloodlines to be a great quarterback for a long time (see page 172).

The Next Thirty

#29
The little-known Friedman (right), is the only player from the 1920s on our list; he threw 66 touchdown passes in his career, more than anyone else in the first 20 years of the NFL.

The next thirty

21. **Doug Flutie**
22. **Y.A. Tittle**
23. **Bob Griese**
24. **Norm Van Brocklin**
25. **Len Dawson**
26. **Ken Stabler**
27. **Warren Moon**
28. **Ken Anderson**
29. **Benny Friedman**
30. **Boomer Esiason**
31. **John Hadl**
32. **Bert Jones**
33. **Drew Bledsoe**
34. **Roman Gabriel**
35. **Randall Cunningham**
36. **Mark Brunell**
37. **Jim McMahon**
38. **Greg Cook**
39. **George Blanda**
40. **Jim Plunkett**
41. **Frankie Albert**
42. **John Brodie**
43. **Dave Krieg**
44. **Frank Ryan**
45. **Ron Jaworski**
46. **Bernie Kosar**
47. **Steve Grogan**
48. **Eddie LeBaron**
49. **Archie Manning**
50. **Peyton Manning**

You will look at the first name and the last name on this list and perhaps kick the coffee table on which the volume is supposed to rest.

Doug Flutie.

Peyton Manning.

That's the fun of this book: I make the rules!

With apologies to Fran Tarkenton, Flutie is the most exciting quarterback ever, and I choose to compensate him for his eight years in exile in the Great White North, not penalize him. Make no mistake about it: Flutie's time in the Canadian Football League *was* forced exile, because NFL teams, foolishly, believed a 5' 10" quarterback could not win consistently in pro football. In his eight years in the CFL, Flutie was MVP of the league six times. His team won the championship three times. I marvel at Flutie as the century closes. Had he played 15 years in the league, we might be talking about him as a member of the NFL pantheon right now. I'd pay luxury-box prices to watch him every week, and I can't say that about any other current NFL player.

"I knew he could play in our league," said Buffalo director of pro personnel A.J. Smith, who convinced the Bills to sign him for peanuts in 1998. "I was lucky that I had an organization that wasn't stigmatized about his height and all the Canadian records. When he was gone for all that time, it was basically, 'Out of sight, out of mind,' as far as the NFL was concerned. Now, any-

#24
One of the top gunners of the 1950s, Van Brocklin (right), once passed for 554 yards in a game, still the NFL record.

#30

Esiason (above) was one of the sharpest quarterbacks of his day; he handled Sam Wyche's weighty playbook with aplomb in Cincinnati.

#22

The Giants' Tittle (right) played with verve and skill and ranked with the best in an era chock-full of greats such as Graham, Unitas and Layne.

body can see he belongs in our league."

Smith spoke in 1999, just after the Bills lost a game in Seattle. Bad field position, horrible play in the defensive secondary and poor special-teams play gave the Seahawks a 23–0 lead. Flutie threw 50 passes that afternoon, completing 24. Buffalo lost 26–16, but three or four times the crowd gasped at Flutie's exploits. Once he left three Seahawks literally grasping air as he faked them out on a 17-yard run. When he had to run, he ran. When he had to pass, he completed big ones. His versatility was his greatest weapon. "If we could have played this game in a phone booth," said Seattle defensive end Michael Sinclair, the defending NFL sack champion, "I could have caught Flutie. Maybe."

Two weeks later I went to Washington to do a story on the Redskins, and I kept hearing their defensive guys talk about how they would keep Flutie in

The cerebral Griese (right) ran Don Shula's offense in Miami to perfection—literally; he capped off the only undefeated season in NFL history by leading the Dolphins to a 14–7 win over Washington in Super Bowl VII.

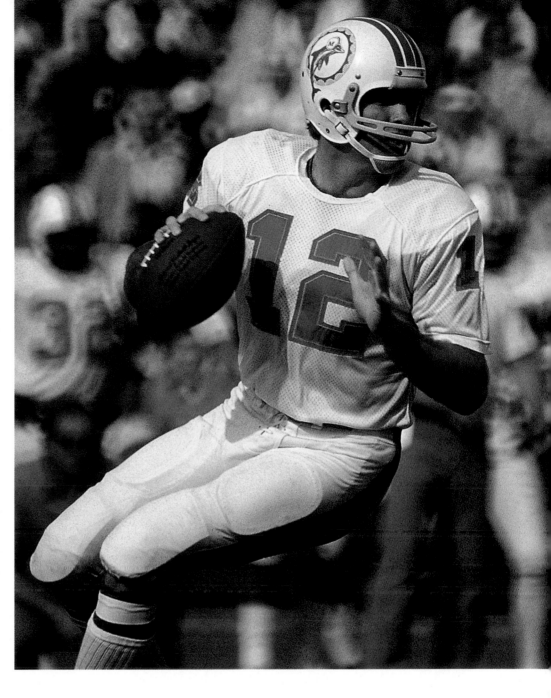

the pocket, bat down all his passes and clog his rush lanes. He wouldn't beat them. That's what every team says about Flutie, and about one in four succeed. In the game against Washington, which was leading the NFC East, Flutie passed for 211 passing yards and scrambled for 40 more as Buffalo won 34–17. The next week, against AFC East leaders Miami, he led a 23–3 rout of the Dolphins, whose defense was rated second in the league at the time. "Pretty easy day," Flutie said.

Now for Manning. Make that the Mannings: Archie, the father, is No. 49, and Peyton, the son, is 50. I consider Archie Manning the best quarterback ever to play for a perennial loser. Ponder his plight: He played for the former expansion-team Saints in 1971 when expansion teams were forced into five or six years of futility by the awful dispersal drafts and no free-agency. Manning the elder watched as nearly every decision the Saints made turned rotten. What luck. A year earlier, Terry Bradshaw, out of Louisiana Tech, went first overall in the draft to a consistent loser, Pittsburgh. Great defense and solid coaching turned the Steelers into four-time Super Bowl winners before the end of the decade.

Manning, for his part, was the No. 1 pick in the draft out of Ole Miss in 1971, also going to a consistent loser. But the Saints never got anything going anywhere, from the front office down to the field. The coach on hand when Manning was selected, J.D. Roberts, had been hired straight out of the Continental Football League, a little-known minor league. But Manning persevered, and at 29, started a run of three excellent seasons, completing more than 60% of his passes and gaining more than 3,000 yards in each year.

Peyton Manning is the most precocious quarterback to enter the NFL since 1983, when John Elway and Dan Marino burst onto the scene. Marino played exceptionally well during his first two seasons, but remember that

#27

If you include his years in Canada, Moon (left) is the most prolific passer in professional football history; if you don't, he still checks in with an impressive 49,097 career yards through the air.

#40

The tenacious Plunkett (above) shook off dismal spells with New England and San Francisco to lead Oakland to Super Bowl glory following the 1980 and '83 seasons.

Miami was a division champion when he came aboard. No quarterback in history has had an opening 25 games like Manning's while leading a bad team out of the wilderness: 6,258 passing yards, 43 touchdown passes. The most impressive stat? He had taken each and every offensive snap of those 25 games. "I've never been so impressed watching a quarterback," said former Raiders coach John Madden after he watched Manning dismantle Dallas 34–24 in

1999. Never? "Never," Madden said. Buffalo defensive coordinator Ted Cottrell said, "He's going to take Marino's spot in this league."

The bottom line: If I can put the tragic Greg Cook of Cincinnati in here—No. 38, because he was the best raw talent with the best arm in the league before shoulder surgery killed his career after two seasons—then Peyton Manning deserves a place too.

Y.A. Tittle and Norm Van Brocklin,

Nos. 22 and 24, were probably the fourth and fifth best passers (behind Graham, Unitas and Layne) after World War II and before Vietnam. Tittle was prolific and courageous, Van Brocklin quick and opportunistic. Bob Griese comes in at No. 23, and I recognize my double-standard here: Griese quarterbacked the only perfect team in modern history, and he guided two Super Bowl winners. Unfortunately for his legacy, he threw 18 passes, combined, in those two Super Bowl wins, and I just can't rank this brainy team player any higher. Len Dawson, who threw 239 touchdown passes in 19 seasons, is No. 25, followed by the wiliest quarterback I ever saw, Ken Stabler.

I struggled over Warren Moon, who has thrown for more yards professionally (in Canada and the United States) than anyone in history, but I think No. 27 is about right for him. His four 4,000-yard passing seasons are impressive, but his numbers are inflated because he played in the pass-happy run-and-shoot offense in Houston.

Ken Anderson, my No. 28, may as well have his picture next to the entry for *efficient* in Webster's dictionary. He completed 70.6% of his passes in 1982, the best percentage ever. After Anderson comes Benny Friedman, the only veteran of the 1920s on this list. Though much more of a runner and an orchestrator than a passer, he threw more touchdown passes, 66, than anyone in the first 20 years of the NFL. Ranked 30th is two-time passing champ and 1988 league MVP Boomer Esiason, who, next to Joe Montana, was the smartest quarterback of the late 1980s. Esiason ran an encyclopedia of a playbook under Cincinnati coach Sam Wyche.

#26

One of the canniest quarterbacks of all time, Stabler (above) made sure that Oakland was a perennial AFC contender in the 1970s.

My final 20 is loaded with potentially controversial choices; I can hear the angry letters being scratched out now. John Hadl, No. 31, threw 244 touchdown passes in his career, more than Bart Starr or Len Dawson. Hadl threw for more yards (33,503) than Sonny Jurgensen. I've got three of today's players ranked closely behind Hadl—Drew Bledsoe is No. 33, and possibly rising since he runs an offense built totally around his talents in New England. Enigmatic Randall Cunningham is No. 35, thanks largely to his season of rebirth, 1998, when he led the NFC in passing and the Vikings to a division title.

Bert Jones, a consummate pocket passer who won a lot of games but was simply too injury-prone to rank higher, is No. 32. Jacksonville's quiet lefthander Mark Brunell—the quarterback most likely to have a career like Steve Young—is ranked 36th. Roman Gabriel, my No. 34, was one of the first classic drop-back passers. The hard-traveled Jim McMahon, who ranks 37th, is one of the greatest gamers ever to play. Cook slides in at No. 38. Mr. Comeback, the ageless wonder George Blanda—who led five fourth-quarter comebacks for the Raiders in 1970 at age 43—comes in at No. 39.

One of the game's great warriors, Jim Plunkett, checks in at No. 40. He overcame tours of duty with terrible teams in New England and San Francisco to lead the Raiders to two Super Bowl titles in the 1980s. The 49ers place four quarterbacks in my Top 50 with the underrated Frankie Albert at No. 41 and John Brodie at No. 42; both had to make do without much help on defense. You may argue with inclusion of the well-traveled Dave Krieg in the Top 50, but I just couldn't ignore the fact that he's eighth alltime in passing yards, and has a touchdown-to-interception ratio of plus-62. He's No. 43. The next five are guys history will view better than the critics of their day did. Frank Ryan and Bernie Kosar are Nos. 44 and 46, keepers of the Cleveland flame with their efficient play. Ryan twice led the NFL in touchdown passes in the era of Bart Starr and Johnny Unitas. Kosar, if not for his nemesis, Denver, would have won two or three AFC titles. The durable Ron Jaworski, who started every Eagles game for a 7½-year stretch, is No. 45, and the battered but productive Steve Grogan is No. 47. The 5' 9" Eddie LeBaron, a Doug Flutie precursor who scurried around the field for Washington and Dallas, is my No. 48.

The father-son duo of Archie and Peyton Manning rounds out the list.

Football fans, start your arguments.

Situation Specialists

Situation Specialists

A man for every situation, and apologies to those who just missed the cut

The wiry Tarkenton (opposite) prolonged his career and frustrated defenses with his elusiveness; the classic drop-back passer Jones (above) was one of the most underrated quarterbacks ever.

There's more than one way to assess a quarterback's impact, much as there's more than one way to play the position. Quarterbacks have come in all shapes and sizes, and they have assumed all manner of approaches to their position. The pudgy but wily Sonny Jurgensen preferred to stay in the pocket and pick out his receivers with laser-like precision. The undersized but equally wily Fran Tarkenton thrived on entropy. He liked to leave the pocket, scramble wildly, and then make something for his team out of the ensuing disorder.

From these contrasting styles it follows that some quarterbacks were better suited to certain game situations than others. Some guys could gun the ball the length of the field if you needed them to, but maybe they weren't so skilled at the touch passes, the timing routes. Some quarterbacks might have seemed asleep at the wheel in the early going, only to become razor sharp when the game was on the line. Other signal-callers were so fleet of foot that they frustrated defenses for their entire careers, gave them one more thing to worry about as they tried to defend their goal line. And some players were so well-rounded, so fundamentally sound without being spectacular, that their overall effectiveness was overlooked. These are the underrated QBs, men like Bert Jones and Ken Anderson.

Before we move on to the situation specialists, a word about my Top 50, and some of the quarterbacks who didn't make it. I have pored over stacks of yellowed newspaper clippings, studied yards of film and plumbed my memories of the hundreds of NFL games I've watched as both fan and reporter. I have compared and contrasted, analyzed and examined, and as I near the end zone of this book, I have to say I'm pretty satisfied with my rankings. The only guy I have a few pangs about leaving out of the Top 50 is Steve DeBerg, and if he's the lone bad call, then I've done my job.

DeBerg played for about 55 teams (actually six), and passed for 34,241 yards in his long and winding road of a career. He threw 23 touchdown passes and only four interceptions in 1990. He was 49ers rookie Joe Montana's onfield tutor in 1979. Undoubtedly, DeBerg, Earl Morrall (Colts, Dolphins) and Don Strock (Dolphins) will go down as the best backups of all time, because when they were called on, they usually came through.

I also took a pass on, in chronological order: Don Hutson's quarterbacks in Green Bay, because there were four who threw to him for significant periods of his 11-year, Hall of Fame career; Bob Waterfield, the first quarterback star in Los Angeles, who just didn't play long enough; Charlie Conerly, one of the Giants' three best quarterbacks ever; Don Meredith, the Dallas quarterback as the Cowboys rose to prominence; Oakland's Daryle Lamonica, the first deep-throwing Al Davis disciple; Buffalo's Joe Ferguson, a gutty strong-armed unsung hero; Joe Theismann, who was almost as good as he thought he was; Cardiac Kid Brian Sipe, who led some terrific drives in a golden Cleveland age; Lynn Dickey and Neil Lomax, who had 4,458- and 4,614-yard seasons for teams that weren't very good; and two productive stars, Jim Everett and Jeff George.

And no, I did not fail to consider Dick Shiner, Rudy Bukich, Larry Rakestraw, Ron Vander Kelen, Milt Plum and Jim Ninowski.

Fellas, you'll have to come back stronger in another life.

StrongestArms

1. **Rudy Bukich**
2. **Brett Favre**
3. **Jeff George**
4. **John Elway**
5. **Jay Schroeder**

Bill Gleason, the veteran sportswriting legend from Chicago, was spinning yarns about the old days of the Bears one afternoon in the Soldier Field press box, and there was one story I found extraordinary.

This was on a Sunday in 1998, and, luckily, I'd been seated next to Gleason for the Minnesota-Chicago game. At halftime, he broke out a corned beef sandwich and a beer from his briefcase and told stories.

"Back in the '60s, the Bears had a quarterback named Rudy Bukich," Gleason said. "Nice fellow. Great arm. And one day, out at practice, he stood at one goal line, wound up, and threw the ball into the opposite end zone. Have you ever heard of anything like that?"

No. Never. The man with the golden gun that most people watch now on Sundays, Brett Favre, went to the made-for-TV Quarterback Challenge before the 1999 season, and won the long-throwing contest with a 71-yard heave. Could someone actually throw the ball 100 yards? "No way," said Phil Simms when I asked him. "Can't be done."

"It's true," said Mike Ditka, who was the Bears' tight end at the time of Bukich's legendary launch. "I saw Rudy do it. I was on the field that day. Now, I'd seen him try it before, and it'd go maybe 95. But he did throw it 100 that one time."

Jack Faulkner, now the administrator of pro personnel for the Rams, has been an NFL coach and scout since 1955. In fact, he was a Rams assistant in 1956 when Bukich returned to football after two years of military service and went to L.A.'s training camp to try to win a job. "Oh yeah," Faulkner said. "Rudy had a gun on him. No question he had the strongest arm I've ever seen. It had to be the strongest ever. He'd come out to practice with us and challenge anybody to a throwing contest. Somebody would take him on, and he'd embarrass

Schroeder (above) winged his way to a couple of fine seasons in Washington, and Favre (opposite) may rifle himself to the Hall of Fame.

the guy. If you were a receiver, he'd burn your hands off."

Bukich kicked around the league from 1953 to 1968 with the Rams, the Redskins, the Bears (he had two stints in Chicago) and the Steelers. He succeeded the aging Bobby Layne in Pittsburgh in 1961, but threw 16 interceptions in eleven games and was dealt to Chicago to back up Billy Wade. George Halas, enamored of the rocket arm, gave Bukich the starting job in 1965, and the quarterback responded with his best season ever: 20 touchdowns and only nine interceptions. You can look it up: The NFL passing leader in 1965 was Rudy Bukich. But after the Bears went 5-7-2 in 1966, Halas dealt Ditka to Philadelphia for the scrambling quarterback Jack Concannon, and Bukich soon took the third seat on the bench—behind Concannon and the eminently forgettable Larry Rakestraw.

"Rifle Rudy, we called him," said Ditka. "I think George decided to go with younger people, and that was it for Rudy." Bukich nips Favre for the Strongarm Title, and the well-traveled Jeff George, who can throw the ball through a brick wall, is third. Then comes John Elway, who once bruised receiver Vance Johnson's gut for a week with the nose of a football, and a surprise—Jay Schroeder, the former minor-league catcher who played for four teams in the 1980s and '90s.

Ditka, a huge fan of Favre's, was asked to compare the arm strength of Favre and Bukich. "I think Brett might be throwing the ball harder this season [1999] than I've ever seen a ball thrown," said Ditka. "But for the distance and the velocity, I don't think anyone could top Rudy."

Strongest Arms

MostUnderrated

1. Ken Anderson
2. John Hadl
3. Bert Jones
4. Archie Manning
5. Frankie Albert

Hadl (above) guided San Diego to two AFL title games, led the league in passing yards three times and in touchdowns twice; Jones (opposite) had just begun to fill Unitas's shoes when shoulder injuries shortened his career.

Paul Brown got lucky. The architect of the newly-formed 1946 Cleveland Browns was fortunate enough to have found the greatest quarterback of all time (in our humble opinion) in a Chicago suburb, and one discovery of rare talent in an Illinois town should have been enough for a lifetime, right? Otto Graham served Brown's Browns well, leading Cleveland to the championship game of its league 10 times in his 10-year career, with seven titles to show for it.

Then Brown, before his fourth season with his second NFL franchise, the Cincinnati Bengals, discovered a quarterback from tiny Augustana College in Illinois. Ken Anderson was the Bengals' third-round pick in 1971, a heavy-legged, pocket passer who immediately showed a precocious poise and all-business demeanor on the field. He reminded Brown of Graham.

Anderson was the smartest guy on the field and like Graham, he never minded when Brown shuttled in plays using messenger guards. He was an unselfish leader who never cared if he threw for three touchdowns or his running backs ran for three touchdowns— as long as the Bengals got the touchdowns. One more thing: Anderson had a decent quarterbacks coach in those days. A fellow named Bill Walsh.

In his second year as a starter, 1973, Anderson, with an average supporting cast, led Cincinnati to the AFC Central title, holding off the nascent Steelers dynasty.

Other than two injury-plagued seasons, he was a consistent 60% passer for the rest of the decade, and then he hit his peak in the early 1980s. He threw 29 touchdown passes and only 10 interceptions in Cincinnati's Super Bowl season of 1981, and completed an NFL-record 70.6% of his passes in 1982. A

measure of the respect his peers had for him came on road trips to Pittsburgh during the 1970s. Anderson always played well and valiantly against the Steelers, and his opponents, in a display of rare respect, invited him into a quiet room for a postgame beer. "Ken Anderson was always a guy who gave us trouble, no matter what we threw at him," said Steeler linebacker Jack Lambert.

Cincinnati being a small city and Anderson being a small-town guy (as well as a downright boring interview), he never got the respect—outside of Pittsburgh and Cincinnati, perhaps—that he deserved. It didn't bother him for a second. He had an outstanding career. He won four conference passer-

rating titles and had a higher completion percentage than Joe Montana in 1982 and 1983. Beyond his impressive stats, Anderson kept the Bengals respectable for years when their personnel was less than All-Pro.

John Hadl, who threw more touchdown passes than anyone in football from 1965 to 1968, absorbed all of San Diego coach Sid Gillman's prodigious offensive philosophy and played better than he had a right to for the Chargers and Rams. He's second on this list.

Bert Jones, Baltimore's more-than-capable successor to Johnny Unitas, led the Colts to three straight division titles in the 1970s, but battled recurring injuries to his right shoulder in

1978 and '79 and never fulfilled his vast potential. Archie Manning, No. 4 in this ranking, was simply born under a bad NFL sign, the Fleur-de-Lys of the New Orleans Saints, and he spent his career trying to revive his horrendous hometown team, an impossible dream. Frankie Albert, who led the All-America Football Conference in touchdown passes in 1948 and 1949, beating out Otto Graham in both years, comes in fifth in our standings of the underappreciated. Albert had a passer rating of 102.9 for San Francisco in 1948, and to tell the truth, many fans probably don't underrate him—because they've never heard of him. Now they have.

MostUnderrated

MostMobile

1. Fran Tarkenton
2. Doug Flutie
3. Steve Young
4. Eddie LeBaron
5. (tie) Jim Zorn
   Randall Cunningham

Tarkenton (opposite), the great improviser, was the original scrambling man; Cunningham (above) made linebackers look silly with his elusive outside moves.

The turning point in the Buffalo Bills' 1998 season was a play kids have been drawing up in the dirt on playgrounds all over America for decades. The quarterback fakes it to the running back, everybody follows the running back, then the quarterback tucks the ball on his hip and runs as fast as he can toward the corner of the end zone. Doug Flutie did this on the Bills' last offensive play of the game to beat previously unbeaten Jacksonville 17–16. The win made Buffalo 3–3, and demolished the widely held belief that the short QB with the quick feet could be no more than a novelty item in the NFL of the late '90s.

They have been fooling the league for years, these quick-footed, smaller types. "I've been hearing it for years," Flutie said in 1998, when he signed with Buffalo after eight years in the Canadian Football League. "Short guys can't play. They can be schemed to stop the athletic plays. We'll see."

Why do coaches and personnel directors and know-it-all general managers continue to favor the stay-at-home pocket quarterback, a generation after seeing the most effective mobile quarterback in league history, Fran

(but unofficial) championship game between Chicago and Portsmouth, Bears fullback Bronko Nagurski ran toward the line of scrimmage intent on pounding the ball through the defense. Suddenly he stopped and the defense converged on him. That left the best offensive weapon in the game, Red Grange, open, and (this was before the age of the T formation) Nagurski tossed him the winning touchdown pass. Grange wouldn't have been so open if Nagurski hadn't first drawn the Portsmouth defense's attention. Flutie and Tarkenton did the same thing.

The debate continues today. In Dallas in 1999, for instance, some veterans grumbled over the ultra-conservative play-calling of head coach Chan Gailey. They wondered where the innovator from Pittsburgh who made Kordell Stewart a multi-threat player had gone. He'd gone to a pretty standard offense, that's where, because Troy Aikman was about as mobile as Barbara Bush.

The Bills, on the other hand, built plays for the elusive Flutie into their game plan. Buffalo appeared to be going downhill when Flutie arrived; now the Bills are a playoff team again.

All of our picks had their careers prolonged by their feet. Tarkenton, the quarterback rushing leader until 1992, survived with his stick-figure physique by deftly avoiding the big hit. Ditto Flutie and Young, though Young, who

Tarkenton, pick apart defenses for years? Flutie and Steve Young, Nos. 2 and 3 on our list of elusive quarterbacks, have proven for the last 15 years that movement is to be desired, not dreaded in a QB. The great thing about a mobile passer is that he gives an offense more options than the pocket quarterback does. Go back years and years. In 1932, in the league's first

Most Mobile

was not quite as slippery (or as small a target) as Tarkenton and Flutie, was bound to take a few heavy shots as the 49ers drafted fewer and fewer quality linemen in the late '90s. Fourth on our list of daring dodgers is Eddie LeBaron, the king of the moving pocket in the 1950s who averaged 5.1 yards per carry for Washington in '55. LeBaron also went for 5.5 yards per carry for the Cowboys in 1960. And finally, tied for fifth, are Seattle's Jim Zorn and Randall Cunningham of the Eagles and the Vikings. Cunningham made linebackers look foolish with his outside moves, and he was the first in the modern trend of athletic, mobile passers that has yielded guys like Mark Brunell, Steve McNair and Daunte Culpepper. Zorn may seem like an odd choice, but the Seahawks quarterback averaged 4.71 yards per carry for a decade beginning in 1976.

That remains a franchise career record. Zorn was a runner of indominatable will and surprising finesse, and like all of the quarterbacks on this list, he kept defensive coordinators up late at night devising ways to stop him. They haven't found a way yet.

Best in the Clutch

1. John Elway
2. Joe Montana
3. John Unitas
4. Bobby Layne
5. Roger Staubach

This one was an upset.

The winner here easily could have been John Unitas. In the game that launched professional football as we know it, the 1958 NFL championship, Unitas engineered the game-tying and, in overtime, game-winning drives.

The winner here easily could have been Joe Montana. His professional resumé is filled with heroic comebacks against all odds and opponents, starting with a play that has grown into a full-fledged legend with the passing of time,

the famous touchdown completion to Dwight Clark known simply as the Catch. It came late in the fourth quarter of the 1981 NFC championship game against Dallas, with the Niners trailing 27–21. Montana reportedly later admitted that he was trying to throw the ball away. Whatever his intentions, the ball ended up in Clark's hands, the Niners won and advanced to the Super Bowl, and the legend of Joe Cool was born.

I could have picked the late Detroit quarterback Bobby Layne, who special-

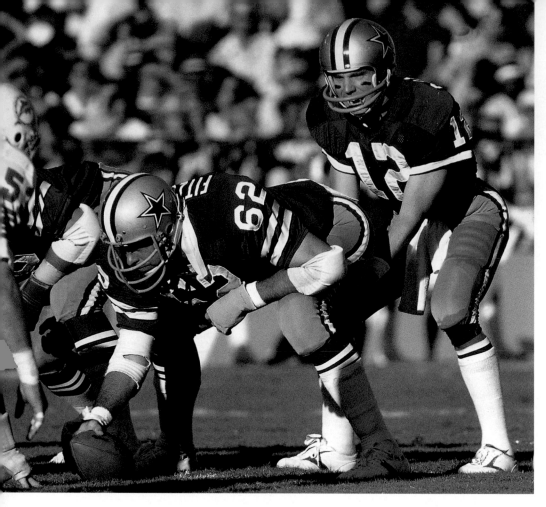

Miracle Makers: Staubach (above), who led Dallas to four Super Bowls, made a career out of rallying the Cowboys from seemingly insurmountable deficits; the résumé of Unitas (opposite) includes clutch performances like the Colts' overtime win against the Giants in 1958.

ized in the two-minute drive with the Lions, winning the 1953 championship game over Cleveland with one. Roger Staubach, who played better the more impossible the situation was, also could have topped this list.

Any of the foregoing could have been the top dog here, but the winner was John Elway, for several reasons. He leads the NFL in fourth-quarter comebacks with 45. He also holds the NFL record for most times sacked (516), from which you can infer that he was making a good number of those comebacks after having his bell rung or his ribs whacked. In 1986 he drove the Broncos 98 yards to the AFC championship over Cleveland, on the road, with the clock winding down.

Elway always had that look in his eyes,

one of certainty more than determination. Jim Fassel, Elway's offensive coordinator in college at Stanford and for two years in Denver, said, "I think he had the best combination of all the things you need to be a clutch player and a great player. The ability, first of all. He was a competitive SOB, more like that than anyone I've ever been around. But he competes relaxed, if you know what I mean. Some guys get so fired up when the game's on the line that their natural greatness can't come through. But John wasn't like that. That truly was the part of the game he enjoyed most, and wasn't jumpy or remotely nervous about it. It got him focused. And I'm telling you, when the players would see that look in his eyes down at the end of a game, the

look that said, 'We are not losing this game,' I think they all snapped to attention, and I think they all played better."

There are many games to choose from as examples of Elway's cool in the clutch. I like Kansas City at Denver, in 1992, when the Broncos trailed the Chiefs 19–6 in the final two minutes of the game. Denver had gone 12 straight quarters without scoring a touchdown. Elway snapped them out of it with a 14-play scoring drive finished off with a 25-yard dart to Mark Jackson. Now Kansas City led 19–13. The Broncos' defense held, and after a long punt return Elway started another drive, this time from the Kansas City 27-yard line. There were 77 seconds remaining. Kansas City defensive end Neil Smith told coach Marty Schottenheimer, "He's gonna do it to us again."

Sure enough, Elway zinged a 12-yard strike to Vance Johnson in the final minute to win the game.

My other personal favorite, is the underrated playoff stunner against Houston after the 1991 season. The Oilers streaked to a 21–6 first-half lead at Denver and clung to a 24–23 lead with 2:07 left when punter Greg Montgomery pinned the Broncos at their own two with a booming kick. Here came Elway. On fourth-and-six from his 28, he scrambled for seven to keep the drive alive. On fourth-and-10 from the 35, the end-zone scoreboard keened THIS IS TENSE. Just the way Elway liked it. He flipped an awkward pass to Vance Johnson, who ran for 44 yards on the play. That led to the winning field goal with seconds left.

"Not my prettiest pass," Elway said of the throw to Johnson, "but it got there."

They usually did. With entire seasons on the line.

Best in the Clutch

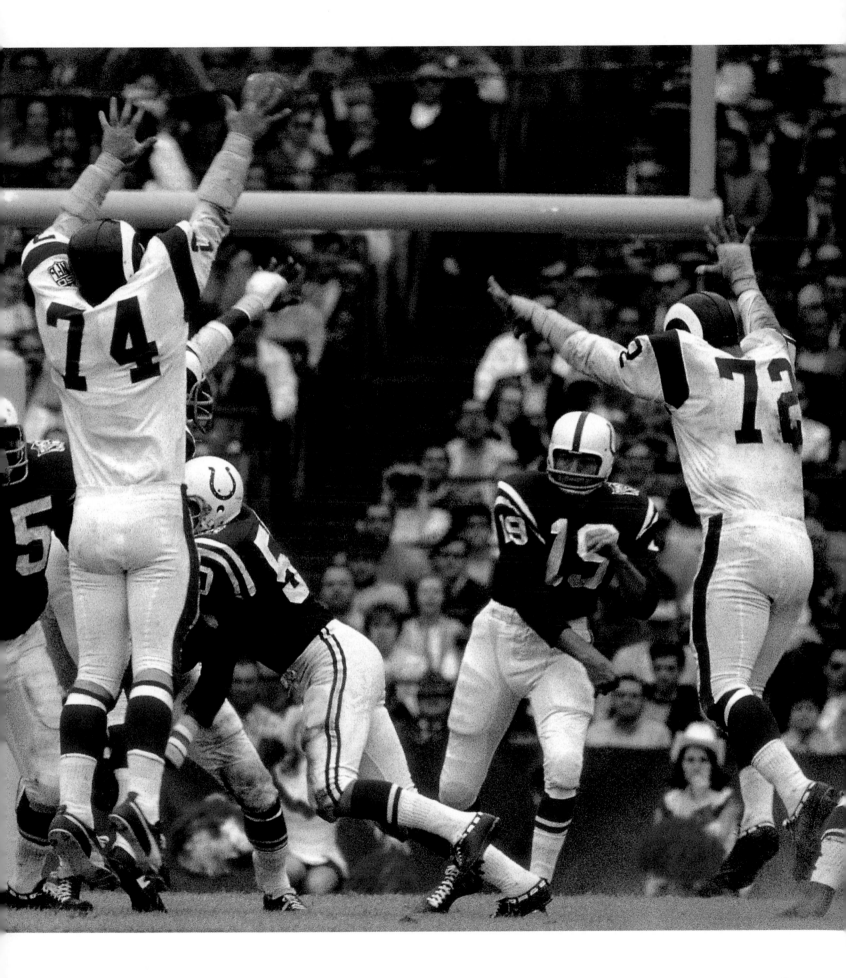

FutureStars

The Young Turks: Plummer (above) who led the Cardinals to their first playoff victory since 1947, reminds many of a young Joe Montana; In 1998, Brees (opposite) set Big Ten records for touchdowns (39) and passing yards (3,983) in a season.

The clock ticks down on Super Bowl LIV in San Diego, and Jeff Hostetler, coach of the Houston Texans, shuts down his handheld electronic play sheet and stuffs it in his back pocket. Just in time. Because jogging off the field toward him, as the press swarms, is his quarterback, the veteran but still excitable Chris Simms.

"We did it!" Simms shouts, throwing his arms around Hostetler and bear-hugging the coach. "We three-peated!"

The year is 2020. The NFL has just concluded its 100th season. Simms, the son of former Giants quarterback Phil Simms, has just led the Texans to their third straight Super Bowl. This—along with his four passing titles and 96.5 career passer rating, the second highest ever, one point behind President Steve Young's career mark—is enough to qualify him as the eighth-best quarterback in our third edition of Greatest Quarterbacks.

President Young, the graying former quarterback, watched this game with Chris's parents in a box high atop Tony Gwynn Stadium. Simms becomes the second quarterback of the last 20 years to make our Top 10. The other, of course, is Peyton Manning of the Colts, who comes in at No. 3. Manning also

won three Super Bowls, between 2000 and 2006, and broke Dan Marino's record for career touchdown passes with 444. He takes his place in the pantheon behind Otto Graham and Joe Montana.

The other impact passers of the 21st Century so far are the Los Angeles Cardinals', Jake Plummer, who delivered the franchise its first conference titles (in 2008 and 2010) since it relocated to Hollywood in 2005. Plummer ranks 14th. San Francisco quarterback Drew Brees, the former Purdue All-America who endured a horrible 9–39 start for the salary-cap-strapped Niners from 2001 to 2003, battled back to win a Super Bowl and two passing titles for his resurgent team.

Cade McNown is the Bears' most popular player since Walter Payton, combining a great zest for the game with superb running and throwing ability. He ranks 24th. Two Viking alums have spots in the Top 30: Daunte Culpepper, who led Minnesota to four straight division championships beginning in 2004, teaming up with the NFL's alltime receiving leader, Randy Moss; and Brad Johnson, our No. 38, a former Viking who won a Super Bowl for owner Daniel Snyder in Washington in 2004.

John Elway's successor, Brian Griese, endured some hard times for the Broncos before breaking through to two straight All-Pro seasons in 2002 and 2003. He's 40th. Two quarterbacks who were college rivals at Louisville and Kentucky in the 1990s, Baltimore's Chris Redman and Cleveland's Tim Couch, both rode 4,000-yard passing seasons early in the century to claim our 43rd and 44th spots, respectively. Number 50? That belongs to Jeff George, who makes it on the strength of his play as the first quarterback of the Texans. In his final season, 2004, a balding George led the Texans to an AFC championship game win over his first team, the Colts.

Predictably, after the 28–27 win over Peyton Manning and Co., George said, "I always knew I was better than Peyton."

Johnson (opposite) revived his career in Washington after injuries chased him out of Minnesota; Manning (above), the first selection in the 1998 draft, improved every week in the pros and broke several rookie passing records.

FutureStars

Photography Credits

Front Cover

Hardcover, clockwise from top left: John Iacono (Elway); John D. Hanlon (Unitas); Richard Mackson (Montana); Heinz Kluetmeier (Staubach); Hy Peskin (Graham); Ronald C. Modra (Marino).

Softcover, clockwise from top left: John Iacono (Montana); Ronald C. Modra (Marino); Hy Peskin (Graham); Heinz Kluetmeier (Staubach); John D. Hanlon (Unitas); John Iacono (Elway).

Back Cover

Associated Press.

Front Matter

Half-title page, Walter Iooss Jr.;
Title page, Walter Iooss Jr.

Introduction

6, John Iacono; 7, Richard Mackson; 8, Ronald C. Modra; 9, Mickey Pfleger; 10, Andy Hayt; 11, Neil Leifer.

1–10: The Elite

12-13, Damian Strohmeyer; 14, Peter Read Miller; 15, John Biever; 16, Hy Peskin; 17, AP; 18, Frank Rippon/NFL Photos; 19, Evan Peskin; 20, Evan Peskin; 21, Corbis/UPI; 22, John Iacono; 23, Andy Hayt; 24, Andy Hayt; 25, Tony Triolo; 26, Richard Mackson; 27, Richard Mackson; 28, Neil Leifer; 29, John D. Hanlon; 30, Neil Leifer; 31, Walter Iooss Jr.; 32, Walter Iooss Jr.; 33, Walter Iooss Jr; 34, AP; 35, Carl M. Mydans/Life; 36, AP; 37, Hall of Fame/NFL Photos; 38, Corbis/Bettmann-UPI; 39, Corbis/Bettmann; 40, Damian Strohmeyer; 41, Damian Strohmeyer; 42, John D. Hanlon; 43, John Iacono; 44, John W. McDonough; 45, Peter Read Miller; 46, John Biever; 47, Al Tielemans; 48, John Iacono; 49, Al Tielemans; 50, Walter Iooss Jr.; 51, Ronald C. Modra; 52, Peter Read Miller; 53, Damian Strohmeyer; 54, Peter Read Miller; 55, Damian Strohmeyer; 56, V.J. Lovero; 57, John Biever; 58, Chuck Solomon; 59, Heinz Kluetmeier; 60, James Drake; 61, Tony Triolo; 62, Peter Read Miller; 63, Heinz Kluetmeier; 64, John Biever; 65, Al Tielemans; 66, Heinz Kluetmeier; 67, Peter Read Miller; 68, Tom Lynn; 69, John Biever; 70, Walter Iooss Jr.; 71, Walter Iooss Jr.; 72, Heinz Kluetmeier; 73, Walter Iooss Jr.; 74, Heinz Kluetmeier; 75, John Iacono.

11–20: They Also Starred

76-77, Al Tielemans; 78, Neil Leifer; 79, John Biever; 80, Hank Walker/Life; 81, UPI/Corbis-Bettmann; 82, AP; 83, Vic Stein/NFL Photos; 84, AP; 85, UPI/Bettmann; 86, Neil Leifer; 87, Walter Iooss Jr.; 88, Neil Leifer; 89, Neil Leifer; 90, Carl Iwasaki; 91, Carl Iwasaki; 92, Walter Iooss Jr; 93, Fred Kaplan; 94, Fred Kaplan; 95, Marvin E. Newman; 96, Walter Iooss Jr.; 97, Fred Kaplan; 98, Peter Read Miller; 99, Al Tielemans; 100, Al Tielemans; 101, Al Tielemans; 102, V.J. Lovero; 103, Al Tielemans; 104, James Drake; 105, Walter Iooss Jr.; 106, Walter Iooss Jr.; 107, Walter Iooss Jr.; 108, Heinz Kluetmeier; 109, Neil Leifer; 110, Ira Block; 111, John Iacono; 112, Corbis/UPI; 113, Corbis/UPI; 114, Neil Leifer; 115, Vernon Biever; 116, Andy Hayt; 117, Andy Hayt; 118, Andy Hayt; 119, Ronald C. Modra; 120, Andy Hayt; 121, Ronald C. Modra; 122, NFL Photos; 123, Transcendental Graphics; 124, Neil Leifer; 125, Hy Peskin; 126, AP; 127, Evan Peskin; 128, Heinz Kluetmeier; 129, John Biever; 130, John Biever; 131, Richard Mackson; 132, Peter Read Miller; 133, Peter Read Miller; 134, Richard Mackson; 135, Ronald C. Modra; 136, Richard Mackson; 137, Andy Hayt; 138, Richard Mackson; 139, Ronald C. Modra.

The Next Thirty

140-141, Heinz Kluetmeier; 142, AP; 143, Daniel Rubin/NFL Photos; 144, John Biever; 145, Neil Leifer; 146, John Biever; 147, Neil Leifer; 148, Richard Mackson; 149, Walter Iooss Jr.

Situation Specialists

150-151, Walter Iooss Jr.; 152, Neil Leifer; 153, Walter Iooss Jr.; 154, Peter Read Miller; 155, John Biever; 156, Jerry Wachter; 157, John Biever; 158, Sheedy & Long; 159, Walter Iooss Jr.; 160, Heinz Kluetmeier; 161, Manny Millan; 162, Peter Read Miller; 163, Heinz Kluetmeier; 164, John W. McDonough; 165, John Biever; 166, Walter Iooss Jr.; 167, John Biever; 168, Heinz Kluetmeier; 169, Walter Iooss Jr.; 170, Scott Troyanos; 171, Peter Read Miller; 172, Chuck Solomon; 173, Damian Strohmeyer.

Index